MAIL ORDER
ON THE
KITCHEN TABLE

*This book is for the beginner who wants to make
MONEY in Mail Order*

Satisfaction Guaranteed
By Marilyn Smith Schultz

TRIBUTE INC. publisher
600 Sunset Drive
McAllen, Texas 78503

𝔗ribute 𝔦nc.

ACKNOWLEDGMENTS

My grateful thanks to the following people for their help, support, and encouragement: Dick Montesi of the DMA Educational Foundation; Tom Milan, Betty Ann Jones, Ron Hartman of The Heritage Group; Lester Rydl with Mr. Computer; Bob McClure of Texas Commerce Bank; McAllen Postmaster Jim Duncan and staff; Tiia Sahni of Nash Direct; Linda Litzenberger of Point West; Mike Moran of R.R. Donnelley & Sons; Jan Seale, my editor; Herschell and Margo Lewis, Fred and Eve Simon, Alan and Liz Drey, Carl and Gilda Samek, Mildred Smith, the Reynoldses, the Kidds, and the Schultzes—especially Karen, Stephen, Elisa, and Frank.

> *...I am the one by whom*
> *This work can best be done, in the right way.*
> *Then shall I see it not too great, nor small*
> *...Because I know for me my work is best.*
> —Henry van Dyke

Library of Congress Cataloging-in-Publication Data

Schultz, Marilyn Smith.

Mail Order on the Kitchen Table.

88-90215
_____ 1988   _____   _____

ISBN 0-9620482-0-8

Printed in the United States of America
by R.R. Donnelley & Sons, Inc.

TRIBUTE INC. publisher
600 Sunset Drive
McAllen, Texas 78503

TABLE OF CONTENTS

PART I: FRONT END ANALYZING

Chapter One
FRONT END ANALYZING:
Careful Does It!

"At last we have a "how to do it" book which makes sense for *anyone* who wants to compete in direct marketing. Marilyn Schultz knows every aspect of selling by mail. She also has the rare talent of being able to condense her vast knowledge into a readable, useful book that leads the reader through the maze of procedures and terminology.

I can't imagine anyone in business considering direct mail and not having this book on the desk. Money-savers, time-savers, frustration-savers, and mistake-avoiders—for the first time they're loaded into one book, written by the expert who opens wide the box of invaluable professional secrets."

HERSHELL GORDON LEWIS
COMMUNICOMP, INC.

INTRODUCTION

Congratulations! You picked up this book, a first step in your success in the mail order business.

Why should you be in direct marketing sales? Very simple: because you want to be. Your motivation is your greatest asset. You have a great idea, you know there are people out there who need it and/or would like it, and you are tantalized by the possibility that they will buy it by mail.

This book then is written for you, a wisher and dreamer, a chance-taker, someone who wants to put to use your creativity, ingenuity, and good old American hustle to get more money and more joy out of life.

Direct marketing starts in dreams and ends in reality. It is an extremely practical, do-able kind of business. Here in this book you will be taken step by step through the process to accomplish your goals. This is a kitchen-table guide to direct marketing sales. Sit down. Have a cup of coffee. Let's get at it. You've got money waiting out there for you.

I married into a direct marketing sales family. Though I had done my share of ordering flower seeds, pet sea monkeys, and barrettes from comic book ads as a child, like most people, I had never considered who was behind my order. As a young adult, I was fascinated by the fact you could talk to your customer on a one-to-one basis and in the privacy of his/her living room. You had the floor—What a deal! You couldn't have much more fun than that!

For years I studied every how-to mail order book I could get my hands on. I went with my husband to meetings of the Direct Mail Marketing Association, as it was called then. (Now it is called DMA). Through these meetings I learned the workings of how to be in and how to operate an entrepreneurial venture.

Then my chance came. After all the years of studying direct marketing sales and going to every seminar I could find, I too was in the direct marketing sales business!

I started perhaps like you will. I made an office in my home. In a different location, I made space for my product and its shipping. In 1974 I opened my business, GALLERY EDITIONS LIMITED INC., a commemorative plate and collectible firm. Some of my clients were the American Rose Society, The International Museum and The American Commemorative Council. Until I sold it in 1985 to become a consultant in direct marketing enterprises, it grew constantly. Today it's still a very successful business, healthy and strong as of this writing.

Like me, you will begin at the beginning, look up years later and find you are the PRO. This, then, is a business you can grow with and learn from. And this book will fit right in with that because you learn from it, in the simplest terms, the best methods of operating your growing business.

This book is different from any other book in the direct marketing sales field: it is for the rank beginner. Technical terms are kept to a minimum. You don't have to feel dumb because you don't know what Front End, Back End, and Continuation are. I also assume you don't have a lot of money to begin with, and that you may not have a separate office or supplies and equipment yet. Salted through the book you will find charts, illustrations, and sample letters to keep you on track.

Let's talk now about the benefits that can come from being in the direct marketing sales business. One of the most obvious is that it's your business. You're the head cheese. You call the shots. And you can call them from almost anywhere. Direct marketing is ideal for parents caring for young children, disabled people, and homebodies. It's great for retirees wanting to utilize a lifetime of work-world expertise. The worker seeking an alternative to his boring 8-to-5 routine, the divorcee who has no outside work experience, the person with a regular job who wants or needs more income—all these may find direct marketing a profitable endeavor. Direct marketing fits as many different lifestyles as there are people.

And the direct sales business can be any size. So many people feel a business has to be big. That simply isn't so. The techniques are the same for all sizes of the business. By cultivating effective management now, you won't have to change any of the business methods when you reach your maximum growth goal. What a deal! In the direct marketing sales business you can have it all.

One of the most exciting things in the direct marketing business will be working with clever, creative people. Using your mind and energy, the sky's the limit on anything you can think up. The direct marketing field provides lots of travel opportunities and satisfaction of a job well done. But most of all, it will give you a good living if you take good care of it.

Introduction

And age has no boundaries here. You can start using this method of business-selling at any age.

You may ask what type of people—besides those with obvious occupational needs already mentioned—get into the direct marketing sales business. Beginning entrepreneurs are people who are not afraid to spend lots of time, energy, and love on their projects. Obviously, they want a challenge and love work. An entrepreneur is a problem-solver, a creator, and a chance-taker. I'd place bets that you are one of these.

When I think of a definition of an entrepreneur, I am reminded of a dear old friend, M.P. Brown. Buster—as we lovingly called him—is dead and gone now, but in his day he was the inspiration for many a potential entrepreneur in the mail order business.

Buster arrived in Fort Worth on a freight train during the oil boom-town days in the late 1930's. He was so young but he had a yen for the big city. When he got off the train, he had no idea where he would go or what he would do. Not long after his arrival, he found work in a chili parlor, a uniquely popular establishment at that time in Ft. Worth. (I can remember getting a bowl of chili with rice there for a quarter early in the '50's.)

The parlors were empty in the late afternoon so Buster got out and made a deal with one of the oil promoters to get investors to put their money into oil speculation. As he so colorfully put it, "There's a mullet born every minute."

He got all the chili parlor employees to help stuff envelopes for the oilman's promotion, using the empty parlor tables as mail counters. ("Work in your own home addressing envelopes! Make a fortune!") From this enterprise, Buster opened the doors to a letter shop, a firm specializing in mailings for other people.

Along the way he picked up one customer who couldn't pay the bill. But he promised Buster that as soon as he made his killing on the mailing, Buster would receive half of the profits. The customer somehow shingled him out of it and Buster never saw his half.

Years later, the same fellow wanted Buster to do an investor mailing. This time Buster was ready for him, but he had to pay in advance. He told him he had just the list for him. He found the Deceased Veterans of Texas list and did the mailing, reporting that, amazingly enough, they didn't have a single response order!

Eventually Buster evolved into the collection sticker business by mail. These were stickers that were stuck on the invoice that a firm would mail out. They would say something like "You are past due.—I'm turning you over to a collections agency." "It is ten days now and I haven't heard from you," etc. And he sold these stickers by mail. The business was successful. Then the business sold to a firm in Iowa. Two young men with the

Iowa firm Martin Baier and Bob Stone came to Texas to pick everything up. The rest is history.

Martin Baier is now with Old American Insurance of Kansas City and Executive Vice President of marketing and Bob Stone became founder of a fine direct marketing agency, Stone and Adler of Chicago.

Another great man in the direct marketing sales business that Buster worked with was Alan Drey, the merge-purge inventor and head of the Alan Drey list firm of Chicago and New York.

You may ask, "Do I fit the profile? Do I dare take the risk?" Before jumping into this new venture, look at the worksheet in Chapter Two that gives you the plan for a profitable mailing with a successful business forecast. So much of your anticipated fear will dissolve after filling in this worksheet. The business is a business of numbers. If you pay attention to the numbers you will know exactly where your business prowess is. Trust your numbers—don't fudge on the worksheet or you are only kidding yourself. Take plenty of time on the mailing forecast and you will cut your risk factor down, down, down. (I'm not going to tell you there isn't some risk involved because there is in anything you do, but there are ways to cut the risk factor—and it's the job of this book to show you those ways.) Work the worksheet over and over again until you have a success on your hands.

In the beginning, you may have to poorboy it, that is, keep it simple and make sure you can afford the project. This book will show you where you can cut corners and where you cannot. It is important to remember that you may have to start small and build as you grow. I always encourage my clients to begin by poorboying it. This way you can find the pitfalls while you can still control the outcome. Some people have all the money they need at their disposal. I caution you not to spend all your investment money initially or start out too large. It is better to do the right testing and growth patterning as I have outlined for you in Chapter Two.

In this connection, I am reminded of a client of mine who had plenty of money for her start-up operation. After I had consulted with her for several months and we had her product, her list, and her promotional materials ready, she wanted to spend lots of money on a beautiful container for her product. I cautioned her not to, even though she could. Here was a place where she could take those extra dollars and get other customers with her mailing piece. The sale was made in the customer's living room— not with the product's container. And our purpose was to be first class with our presentation and to get customers.

She saved her money to reinvest on getting subsequent sales after her first mailing. Her container was not ugly but it was modest, she didn't compromise the quality of her product, and she had money to move forward in the most important part of the business—moving her product. It's in our nature to want to hurry and be big NOW! But start off slow—keep it simple, trust your judgement and the numbers—and you will do fine.

The matter of money always haunts us. What kind of money will it take to do my direct marketing project? It's back to the profitable mailing form, along with another form also in Chapter Two. Here is a chart for determining the price of the mailing cost per thousand pieces of promotional material mailed, based on 100,000 mailing pieces.

Don't spook out now! You don't have to mail 100,000 pieces. But it is a guide to give you some idea of how to scale down the price for what you can afford at this present time.

Many factors come into play here. Perhaps you already have a mailing list to use: in that case, there would be no charge for that section. On the other hand, perhaps you only want to mail 1000 pieces. This, then, is a guide for you to work from that will help you in making a mailing decision based on how much money you have and how much you will need for the mailing. You can also save money by shopping around. In this day and time there are many hungry printer, artist and letter shops that would die for your business. But plan to spend as much money as you can afford for marketing your product only after doing your work sheets. Get the best for the money you will be able to spend. A second-class piece looks like a second-hand piece and your product will never recover. First impressions really do count. You have all the tools in this book to work out most of the questions you can think up. This is not to say you won't want to consult other books and resources. As my business and knowledge of the field grew, I read everything I could get my hands on. No doubt you will want to do the same thing.

After you read each chapter thoroughly and begin to put into practice the methods recommended, your direct marketing techniques and skills will gradually become second nature. You will be surprised how fast you will learn when your money is at stake!

After a while, you will keep the book on your desk and use it to refresh your mind. This book, I hope, will become for you your direct marketing sales bible.

There is no magic in direct marketing sales by itself. You are the one who makes the magic with your excitement and dedication. Dream, and hope, and dare to be called crazy—then work like mad to realize your dreams and hopes and to have the last laugh—all the way to the bank!

In Chapter Seventeen the skills and functions you will need to run your business are spelled out for you. One has so much to think about getting started that this is one area you don't have to dwell on. If you will carefully read over the thirteen skills it takes to run your business, you will find that you can do almost all of them yourself—of course, depending on what size your business is. The beautiful thing about these functions is that as your business grows they are the same thirteen functions you have always had. Perhaps as you grow you will have to have other bodies to carry out the functions but the actual skills are the same.

Chapters Sixteen and Seventeen tell you what skills will be needed, who does each skill and how to do each skill. If you will just trust this method you will make a big leap ahead. In the beginning of my direct marketing business I only had one other person helping me. In fact, it was a typist on a part-time basis. (Ah ha, did you see what I just slipped in on you? That's right. You don't need to hire someone full time if you don't need them full time.)

Snugly tucked away in Chapter Two is the formula for the 1- to 5-year growth pattern. The beauty of this formula is that you can work it around so many ways to fit your needs. Only grow as fast as you can keep up with it. If you follow this simple method you will know from the beginning what your future will be. DIRECT MARKETING is the only method of business I know that you can do that in.

I have in this introduction shared with you some of my love of the direct marketing business, and through my experience and success I will show you how to be successful too.

I have a B.A. in applied music. The organ is my instrument. And I do spend lots of hours on that bench. But my other bench has been at the desk having fun in the direct marketing business and consulting. As I said earlier, I learned as I went along. After 16 years of being in the business I want to pass on to you my experience and success. There is something wonderful and strange about the people in the business: NO one has ever said they wouldn't help me or that it couldn't be done! Everyone was so good to help and solve any problem I could come up with. Now it is my turn to pass on this wealth of information to you.

Chapter One is our first working chapter. As we go along from chapter to chapter, if you at some time feel overwhelmed, go back to where you understood what you were reading, and start from there. Read slowly and take your time. You know it takes lots of planning; do your mistakes on paper first—it's a lot cheaper. You don't need a college degree in direct mail marketing to get into the business. The field has finally caught the attention of the university population: more about that at the back of the book.

Now get that cup of coffee and let's get on with it.

Chapter 1

FRONT END ANALYZING:
Careful Does It!

When you think of starting a business, you naturally have to talk yourself into it. Why, you ask yourself, would anyone want to do business with me by direct mail? The answer is, for the same reasons *you* purchase things by mail.

For more and more adults working fulltime, shopping in stores during their off-hours is a fantasy or a nightmare. When their work day is complete, they want to get home, get comfortable, and spend a non-taxing evening. A mail order mailing piece or catalog and an armchair suit them much better than a pair of sturdy walking shoes, heavy packages to carry, traffic snarls and parking fees, and the risk of being mugged. Why go out?

But ease of shopping is not the only reason there's a place out there for you and your product. Inveterate armchair shoppers almost always like the idea of what I call controlled impulse buying. It sounds like a contradiction in terms but is really not. Here's what I mean. Impulse buying is not necessarily a dirty phrase. Catalogs and other mailing pieces coming into the home suggest to prospective buyers items they didn't know they needed or wanted. This is especially true of gifts. But, you say, so does shopping in a store. Here's where the "controlled" impulsive buying comes in. Direct mail ordering allows the customer not only a smorgasbord of ideas but an orderly means of considering them. There's a rational description, probably a picture, and a delineation of sizes, colors, measurements, or other specifications. A plus of control in mail order shopping is that, with a catalog or brochure from a reputable—even snooty—company in hand, the customer does not have to question his taste. Brooks Brothers is always Brooks Brothers. You're safe with their catalog in your hands.

The customer's right brain loves the surprise element, the impulsiveness, of being shown something wonderful she or he didn't know about.

1

The left brain, the controller, critiques the choice according to the presentation of facts. There's no reason you can't have a mailing that will sell your customer those two camels that are the perfect gift for friend John—provided their hide tones match John's back 40!

There's a special group of direct mail shoppers who would rather do anything than mix with people. They don't like crowds and they don't like salespeople hovering over them. They prefer making up their own minds in the quietness of their living rooms or offices.

Two comments you'll hear in criticism of mail order shopping are that the shopper must wait for the items and that mail orders are more expensive. There's not much you can say to refute the first argument, except to point out that two or three hours spent today tramping through the stores in order to be instantly gratified may be more costly time wise than four days going about one's business while a mail order is processed. Certainly it's possible for mail order items to be more pricey than their equivalents in discount stores, but there are just as many mail order items that are considerably lower in cost than their high-overhead store cousins because the supplier stocks in quantity in a low-rent warehouse.

So you see, the shop-at-homer can be almost anyone, with a variety of reasons for settling down in front of the TV for an evening of shopping. The habitual general at-home shopper is sophisticated, affluent, and educated, with saving time a high priority. He or she is probably an orderly type, with patience to wait for a desired item and a keen eye for value. Many are "Yuppies", "Life-Begins-at-50" empty nesters, and "Dear Occupants"—a great number of people in whose hands the catalogue has landed.

Convenience is by far the biggest draw for direct mail shopping. Sales have exceeded over $50 billion to date with expectations for the amount to be much higher each year.

Now give some hard thought to WHAT you are going to sell. Maybe you already know. Maybe you're reading this book because you have an idea so hot it's too good to keep. The list of mail order products is as long as there are possibilities for human consumption. Food products are record holders in popularity. Then there are clothes, stamps, books, collectibles, sewing projects, art, jewelry, magazines, flowers, plants, stationery, scuba gear, household gadgets, tools, and medications.

We have a friend who sells restoration tools for use at historical sites. Is that specialized or is that specialized! You can imagine how difficult these would be to find in a retail store, but they're all there in Rick's catalog.

In another category are services sold by mail. These include insurance, fund-raising, attorney services, and instruction of all sorts. Remember the famous ad beginning "They laughed when I sat down to play?" That was mail order piano lessons.

What sells is what you find being needed. If you're still searching for SOMETHING to market, make your highest priority that of filling a need, preferably a huge need. In the biz that's known as marketing a product with a large "universe." Your universe is your body of potential customers. How to find your universe and turn it into sales is what this book is about. The product, I feel, to be a real success must be first class. If you are putting lots of money and effort into advertising, then only sell the best products you can find. Sure, there are plenty of people out there who will sell cheap stuff or seconds, but not you. Not only do you want to stay in business, but you want to be proud of the product you are selling your customer.

On several occasions I was asked to merchandise other firms' products; however, I accepted only what I felt was the best. A good reputation will largely determine whether you stay in business. Regardless of popular belief, most people really don't mind paying a slightly higher price for quality products.

If you are going to sell by direct marketing, plan to charge enough money for your product. Otherwise, you shouldn't be in the business. A popular pricing practice in several business fields is to use the keystone pricing equation. A keystone is the actual cost of a product from the wholesaler doubled. To keystone, the merchant doubles the price of a $50 item to $100. For example, a box of pecans costs him wholesale $8.00: if he keystones the retail price of the pecans would be $16.00. In direct mail marketing, sometimes you'll find keystoning but it's more common to charge three to four times the wholesaler's cost. Say the pecans from the wholesaler cost $8.00. In direct marketing sell them for $24.00 up, depending on your marketing expenses and what you feel a customer would pay. Don't be shy. You are in the business to make money and to sell the best product you can find. Try to head for at least a 15% to 20% profit for yourself after expenses have been accounted for.

Other considerations when choosing a product might be whether it is seasonal (like grapefruit or pecans), what products you have some background in or special knowledge about, what country or countries you want to sell in. (I heard the other day a discussion on a call-in radio show in which an Alaskan entrepreneur was asking a financial adviser about the feasibility of selling designer clothes by mail order from Alaska. The adviser was giving him one hard time about the location—and well he should, given the mailing rates, schedules, and accessibility to raw materials.)

At this point think seriously about your most important commitment in this venture (besides the one to yourself to make money!). Your major effort will be to win and keep your customer. You must understand from the outset that your sincere dedication to finding and pleasing your customer is the catalyst that will make you money. SERVICE IS THE

KEY. The man who cashed in on the service idea was Aaron Montgomery Ward in the year 1872.

If you are not at ease with people in social situations, take steps now to improve your social skills. You will need to be friendly and kind to your customers, letting them talk to you as though you had nothing else to do. True, it's in the nature of direct mail marketing that you will never meet most of your customers face to face. The telephone fills this gap so brush up on your telephone-ese, both manners and presentation, in preparation for communicating with your customers.

You'll need to exercise your powers of persuasion to show your prospective customer how your product is unique and timely, and how you intend to back up the quality with a guarantee or warranty. A guarantee tells the customer how much time he/she has to return the product. There are three favorite types: 15 days, 30 days, or one year. You'll need to be able to assure your customer of speedy and safe delivery. These skills not only sell your product initially but assure you years and years of loyal customers.

One of my favorite stories about the vagaries of communication in this field involves a direct marketing attorney. This delightful man deals in space ads: "Let me get your invention patented for you." Well, he tells me that he rarely sees a client in person. However, on one occasion a man wrote that he could only explain his invention in person to the attorney.

Reluctantly, the attorney consented. The inventor arrived and spread his carburetor idea all over the attorney's desk. When the hopeful man paused for breath, the attorney asked, "Why is this carburetor going to get 200 miles per gallon when a regular one won't?"

"That's easy," replied the inventor. "God's going to make these for me."

What could he say? The attorney reported he whirled around in his chair, away from the poor man, and bit his lip to keep from laughing. Sometimes it doesn't pay to meet your client face to face!

One last thing to bring to your attention is, what are to be your business ethics? You may think it a silly question, but is it? I have found that if you think about what your ethics will be in the market place and how you want to be treated and your impression and ideals that will come across to the customer, you are ahead of the game. Are you going to be honest and forthright? Are you going to believe your customer? Do you plan to pay your bills on time? Think about it. What is your attitude about your employees' behavior? Are you going to allow sexual discrimination? Will you allow sexual harassment? Being late on the job? Sick pay days? What will you tolerate from them? (Notice I'm suggesting you're going to have some employees eventually.) What do you expect from yourself?

You will have your own set of stories—funny and otherwise—to tell after a while in this game, but most of your customers will be interesting, sincere, intelligent people who will appreciate your supplying them with a needed product or service. A few of them you will meet in the course of your business—at conventions, shows, gatherings of like-minded individuals. And if you are a people person, you will thoroughly enjoy these opportunities to get to know personally one of the names on your card file or in your computer.

Chapter 2

DECISIONS! DECISIONS!
More Upfront Thinking

In Chapter One we philosophized about what a customer is, what sells, and what it takes to keep your customer. In Chapter Two we are going to discuss how to sell the product. First, a short course in kinds of mail order services. Business categories are 1. Service Firms, 2. Users: Consumer Products and Services, and 3. Users: Business/Industrial Products and Services. How these categories should be marketed is your next basic decision. Do you use for your advertising—mail, radio, TV telephone 800 selling, co-oping, catalogues, brochures or space ads? Do you want to sell to the private home, or business-to-business? Let's begin by listing some suggestions by categories as they are listed in the Direct Marketing Association directory.

1. Service Firms

Advertising agencies
Sales promotion
Creative consultant
Marketing consultant
Management consultant
Fund-raising agency
Fund-raising consultant
List brokers & compilers
List managers
Telephone marketing services

Cable TV
Direct Marketing Media
Fulfillment services
Print services
Computer services
Information services
Paper mills and distributors
Private delivery service
Lettershop
Printers etc.

2. Users—Consumer Products and Services

Consumer service (including public utilities)
Consumer products—manufacturers

Decisions! Decisions!

Consumer products—etc. wholesalers and distributors
Consumer non-profit organizations
Consumer non-profit associations, societies and educational
Consumer financial services (includes banks, savings & loans)
Consumer insurance
Consumer products include space, TV etc.
Consumer mail order products
Catalogues
Clubs and continuity programs
Consumer periodical publications
Publishers
Trade books
Retail stores having a separate mail order division

3. Users—Business/Industrial Products & Services

Industrial services—travel
Transportation
Public utilities
Manufacturers
Wholesalers
Distributors and dealers
Business equipment
   manufacturers and distributors
Premium/incentive suppliers
Financial services—
   commercial banks

Promoting to business users
Insurance
Catalogs
Periodical publications
Trade papers
Books
Records directories
Training programs
Commercial banks
Credit verification

You see that you have a wide range to work from. This book deals
with a small section of this vast sea of opportunities — direct mail or 2)
Users—consumer products & services. However, from time to time, all
three areas may concern us. For example, let's say we are selling china by
mail. We would be classified under Section Two. However, our firm may be
using an advertising agency, which is under Section One. Perhaps we will
use five or six of the service groups to get our product to the customer.
Section Three: Users—Business/Industrial Products & Services is very
popular today because it feeds people who want to work in the business-
to-business field. In other words, this group only want to work with businesses, not with the individual consumer in direct marketing. Another
way to state this is that Section Three is a supplier to Section Two, which
is in direct marketing sales. Here again, if we are classified under Section
Two but we are considering a premium/incentive for our customer, we
would be working hand in hand with Section Three, the user-business

group. For example, a client of mine was beginning a new fruit business and so for a premium/incentive, four serrated spoons were placed in every box of fruit that was purchased. It clearly increased sales. Many of the same techniques we will be using for direct marketing are also used in the business-to-business field. The main difference is that in the second field you are dealing with a person on a one-to-one basis and with Section Three you are dealing as one business to another business. Actually Two and Three are fed from One. Neither consumer products or business/industrial can work without the service firms. Each has wonderful benefits that will be helpful just for you to promote your product. So any way you go, you will be using all three divisions.

Now that you know how you are going to get help in preparing your mailing piece, it is time to choose your advertising channel.

Will it be totally direct mail? Will you use a combination of direct mail, telephone marketing, co-oping, catalogues, or space ads?

Much will depend on how much money you have to spend, and what will reach your market for the smallest cost with the greatest returns.

In using the space ad approach (which means you take out an ad in a magazine to promote your product), it is very difficult to break even. I know people swear you can make it on that alone, but most people I have dealt with over the years simply don't make a huge profit. I feel the reason to use space ads is to get your product out to the general public for credibility. Rented lists are so specialized that you can't reach everyone. A space ad fills the void.

If you can't afford an ad on your own then there is a wonderful device called co-oping. That means that several people are in the same boat and so advertising companies will take your ad and combine the ad with another company and split the cost of the advertising, making it cheaper for both companies. On the other hand, it can also mean that when the magazine is running slow on ads, it can fill in with yours. This will cut your advertising cost as well. Your ad runs a bit cheaper that way and you might break out (pay for your ad).

I LOVE THE TELEPHONE . . . We'll talk more about it in office telephoning in Chapter Seven. I will say at this point that "office telephoning" calls are known as warm calls. When a customer receives your mailing piece and he calls into the office with an order, he has not been "invaded". They call you because they want the product. The type of calls you will use for marketing are called COLD CALLS or invasive calls. A cold call is when you rent a list and call these people cold. They have never heard of you before. Cold calls are a nice back-up to your product. The cold call procedure is tested just like your mailing will be. If you use a firm, they will be able to tell you in 25 hours whether or not telephone marketing will work for you. If they report positive, telephone marketing can get underway. And the testing firms then mail you these orders for your company to process. Although this is certainly a method you can employ for yourself, I must tell you it is a lot of work. Testing companies are set up to handle the calls professionally. Oftentimes, the companies will use out-of-work actors to call because they have happy smiles in their voices. The average calls to get one order can run from 20 to 25 calls.

Television 800 sales are tested as well. An ad for television can run you from $25,000 on up. Then it will take around $25,000 to do the telephone backup. This is a different use for the telephone. The orders are coming off the TV ads. A 5-city group or section of the country will be tested. If positive, the ads will be expanded over the country.

In direct marketing everything is tested first. That's the secret of your success. No matter how big or small your firm or company is, it is all in the numbers.

There are methods to help you decide which direction in direct marketing you may want to go. Or you may have decided that you only want to use direct mail. I think that's the way to get started. Get one direction in the direct marketing field going and then experiment with the other methods. There are surveys to help you decide on a product and whether or not it will be successful. Heritage House of Nashville, Tenn. checks out each new product they have in mind with a survey. They ask their customer what they want. If you don't have customers yet, rent one list you think will work for you and mail a survey to a few of the names on the list and see what kind of feedback you get. You may have a few surprise answers. There are research groups that do a feasibility study and they test, test, test the product. In the shopping malls you may have seen people taking a poll on a product.

Now that we have touched on what to sell, and how to sell it, let's talk about where you will get your start-up money.

Do you already have a banker? Do you know one? The banker and bank you choose now will be your mainstay through thick and thin. Ask the banker you interview if he/she has ever had any dealings in the direct marketing field. There are many bankers who know and understand direct marketing. And you might have to interview several before you find one you feel comfortable with. You may have lots of money you can get your hands on without using a banker, but that is really rare. So you had better take time and find a banker who will let you see or talk to him/her when you need $ in a hurry. I also advise you to get a banker who has authority. So many times a person will go to a lender who can make small loans, but when a crunch comes along, this individual just can't help you out. Find a banker from the beginning who can loan you what you need.

I predict that when you do your homework (making your five-year-plan) and take it to the banker, you will have a lot of cooperation from the banker. If you will set up a loan amount you think you need before you get on your feet, then only borrow what you need at the time, it will save your having to go back and back to ask for more. That way you have the money available.

There are some terms that go along with money that you will need to know: "Accounts receivable," "accounts payable," "financial statement," "line of credit," "letter of credit." Let's start with accounts receivable. I'm reminded of a dear friend who started a small direct marketing firm from her home. She is a writer and her husband is a composer. They put together a series of children's books with music to market to schools. After a few months in business, the bank called for a financial report. Well, she took everything she could to the banker to show him how well she was doing. After quite a long session he asked to see her accounts receivable. She kept looking over all the papers she had brought with her and with her head down remarked, "I know it is here if I just knew what it was."

Let's learn from her experience. "Accounts receivable" is the amount of money your customers owe you for the sale of your product.

Another term you need to be at ease throwing around is "accounts payable." That's what you owe your suppliers. The financial statement is a complete financial picture of where your business is. It should include:

> your assets such as cash on hand
> accounts receivable
> fixed assets (office equipment, accumulated depreciation)
> other assets
> liabilities (payroll taxes, accounts payable)
> long term liabilities (bank notes,etc.)
> equity (capital stock, retained earning, current net income)
> income (from sales of your product)
> cost of goods sold (net income before operating expenses)
> operating expenses (such as auto expenses, bank charge, credit expense, depreciation, etc.), and net income.

Next is a line of credit. We touched on that briefly when we talked about setting up a one-time loan to be borrowed against with the understanding that if you miscalculated you could borrow some more. All of us think that can't happen, but I promise you it can. As well as we plan, sometimes Murphy's Law intervenes. A product doesn't get to you when promised, you need a few more people to do the job and so on. So setting up a line of credit is essential to your business health. What is a letter of credit? It is your banker promising that when you order a product out of the country that the foreign supplier will be paid—often out of your existing bank account or a loan the banker will make to you. This is frequently used because of the difference in foreign currency, or your lack of credit with that firm yet. They want assurances that they will be paid and can you blame them? That's what we all want, to be paid.

Now, the business loan. Be sure you shop around. Each bank has a different prime rate, and some banks have one loan percentage borrowing fixed rate while other banks have floating rate loans. Prime rate is a rate of interest that commercial banks charge for short-term loans to their most credit-worthy corporate customers. Prime Rate serves as a basis for setting other higher rates: it is usually the lowest interest rate available. In times of inflation, the prime rate goes up, and as inflation subsides, it goes down. That means whatever the bank has to pay for borrowing its money, you will pay either 1 or 2 percent higher above prime when you borrow it. And that 1 or 2 percent can go as high as from 9 to 20% of the total loan rate if it's a floating rate and not a fixed rate—so be careful. I might add here, a friend of mine was helping her husband out "down at the office" by paying the interest on a loan he had borrowed. Was she proud! Until she discovered you pay interest every day, not just once. Remember interest on your loan is charged to you each and every day.

You might also want to set your payment on your loan to be after a big season, once a month, or twice a year. Work out what will work best for you. Remember, banks are in the business to rent money, so the bank should do what you need to work best for you.

Oftentimes, banks will want collateral. Collateral means security, such as stocks or bonds, given to a creditor to guarantee the discharge of an obligation by the debtor (you) in the purchase of goods on credit. Frequently the goods themselves are the collateral, as in the credit purchase of a car. That means in case you can't make the payments they will get their money back. This procedure is being used more and more due to the high bad debts the banks have had to eat the last few years. So don't be upset if they ask you for collateral. It's just business, nothing personal.

What type of accounts are you going to want to have, once you have received your loan? You will need a general account out of which you will pay for your supplies and your products from the wholesaler or manufacturer, as well as make your loan repayment. Remember you hope someday to have employees, so with that in mind perhaps it would be good to have a payroll account. You can have several accounts under your one bank account number, just different divisions to make your business run smoother. Another division could be a refund account.

Once you know where your money is going to come from, you will need to find an attorney. Virtually, the process is the same as with getting a banker. Get to know a good attorney. In the set-up stage of your business, it shouldn't cost too much or take a long time to accomplish this. But here again you need to get an attorney who knows you don't have much start-up money and will charge you accordingly. You just have to shop around for one with whom you have rapport. Then decide what form your business should be in. There are four main areas: 1) sole proprietorship, 2) corporation 3) partnership (which includes a general or a limited) and 4) a sub-chapter "s" election. You will have to review these with your attorney to see which best fits your tax situation. Once you have made your decision, the forms will need to be sent to the Secretary of State for approval. At this time he will assign you a tax number. This number is what you will use for all your business transactions.

While you're setting up the legal forms for your new business you may want a trademark, patent or copyright as well. You will need a different type of attorney called a patent attorney. There are many fine ones in Washington, D.C. The cost for a trademark or copyright runs around $500.00. The beauty of owning such is that your name is protected by law. No one else can use the name for advertising products. So it really is worth the investment.

A patent is something else. Patents are governed by Title 35 United States Code and in general, protect the invention or discovery of any new and useful industrial or technical process or any new and useful improvement thereon. Here, you are talking about a lot more time and money. A patent can take as long as 3-5 years to secure and cost you about $5,000.00. There are many searches that have to be made and a lot of reading and digging work. But if you can get one, it's great. We have a couple of inventions and patents in our family. Being in direct marketing, my husband Frank had a great idea. Why not put your advertising piece in a plastic envelope so that your art would be seen right away and it would grab the receiver's attention? Well, he got the patent. But we couldn't get anyone to produce it. A company in Colorado said they would see what could be done; however, the financial payment to us would be nothing for six months. We were so desperate we went with them. When the six months' time was up, they wouldn't continue with the deal. What a deal— not even for free. Then a few months later another company decided they would invent the same idea. While going through the patent office they ran into Frank's idea. So a good marriage was made. That envelope is still used today. You receive many magazines etc., in it (such as Reader's Digest).

Another example: While actively in the plate business I found that corrugate was just not strong enough to ship plates in. So I invented a styrofoam shipper as a protection for the china. I received the patent and it too is in use today. By our getting the clearance and patent, our china breakage went from 300 for every 5000 to 1 in every 5000. Savings of re-manufacturing resulted, plus happy customers received their plates in one piece. So it can be done.

If you want to follow up on either a patent or a copyright, here are two addresses:

Commissioner of Patents and Trademarks
Washington, D.C. 20231

Register of Copyrights
Library of Congress
Washington, D.C. 20540

Now that you have your banker in mind, and your attorney, it's time to look at what you really are going to need financially to get this new business off the ground. I have prepared the following charts along with information I have collected through the years. One Direct Marketing ba-sic institute, a four day intensive course on direct marketing methods, conducted by Freeman Gosden had the hand-out for the students entitled "Worksheet for Planning Profitable Mailings." It was in a form that was concise and easy to read. It also covers most everything that I do in prep-aration before a mailing. I even go into a bit more detail so I have added additional items. I just want you to know how valuable a basic institute can be. Each time I attend these sessions I learn something new. After be-ing in the business for 15 years that's saying something. Since most of you won't attend a basic institute, I'll bring as much information to you as I possibly can through this book.

Earlier in the chapter we discussed taking your five-year plan to your banker . . . just fill in the blanks in the charts below and you will have all the information you'll need to take with you.

You shall have success!

The charts are:

Worksheet for a profitable mailing
Direct marketing math
Five-year-plan
Matrix for determining cost per thousand mailed

WORKSHEET FOR PLANNING PROFITABLE MAILINGS

1. Selling price of merchandise or service _____

2. Cost of Filling the Order _____
   a. Merchandise or Service _____
   b. Royalty _____
   c. Handling Expense (drop shipping and order
      processing) _____
   d. Postage and Shipping Expense _____
   e. Premium, including Handling and Postage _____
   f. Sales tax if any (1 × 6%) _____
   g. Container for shipping _____
   Total cost of Filling the Order _____

3. Administrative Overhead
   a. rent/light/heat/maintenance/credit checking/
      collections etc. (10% of #1) _____

4. Estimated Percentage of Returns, Refunds or
   cancellations _____

5. Expense in Handling Returns
   a. return postage and handling (2c + 2d) _____
   Total cost of Handling Returns _____

6. Chargeable cost of returns (10% of line above) _____

7. Estimated Bad Debt Percentage _____

8. Chargeable cost of bad debt (#1 × #7) _____

9. Total variable cost (#2 plus #3, #6 and #8) _____
   (product, administration, cost of returns and bad debt)

10. Unit profit per order (#1 less #9) _____

11. Return Factor (100% less #4) _____

12. Unit profit per order (#10 × #11) _____

13. Credit for returned merchandise (10% of #2a) _____

14. Net profit per order (#12 plus #13) _____

15. Cost of mailing per 1000 _____

16. Number of orders per 100 needed to break even (#15
    divided by #14) _____

17. Number per thousand (#16 × #14) net profit per order _____

MAIL ORDER MATH

Percent of Return = $\dfrac{\text{NUMBER OF ORDERS} \times 100}{\text{TOTAL NUMBER PIECES MAILED}}$

Example: If you mail to 100,000 prospects and receive 2000 orders, your rate of response is 2%

How many orders do I have to get to get 2%?

Advertising Cost per order = $\dfrac{\text{Total cost of Mailing}}{\text{Number of orders received}}$

Example: You send out 100,000 mailing pieces at a cost of $275 per thousand pieces (total $27,500)
You receive 4000 orders.
$\dfrac{\$27000}{4000}$ = $6.88 cost of each order

FORMULA FOR A DIRECT MARKETING FIVE YEAR PLAN
THAT YOU CAN TAKE TO THE BANK
EXAMPLE BASED ON MAILING 125,000 ADVERTISING PIECES

NUMBER OF PIECES MAILED   125,000

RESPONSE	NUMBER OF CUSTOMERS
.002	250
.003	380
.004	500
.005	625
.006	750
.007	875
.008	1000
.009	1125
.010	1250

Your response will be based on how good your mailing piece is, your choice of the proper list, and the advertising copy. Each list that you have mailed will respond differently. You will end up with a response called a mean average. For example, let's say ABC list brings in a response of .004 and DEF list brings in a .01 response. Each list is checked against itself.

The ABC list mailed 5000 pieces: your response is 20 customers. You will now divide the 20 customers by the 5000 pieces of mail...your response then is .004. That is a true average. When you have finished dividing each list against its responsé, you will then add up all customers you received against the 125,000 piece mailing. This is the mean average. You may have an all over mean average of .007. For the example below I will use an .008 mean average because copy, list, and advertising piece appealed to the reader...it worked. The gross product cost to the customer will be $24.95.

EXAMPLE OF .008 RESPONSE

COST OF PRODUCT TO THE
   CUSTOMER $24.95

$125,000 \times .008 = 1000$ CUSTOMERS

1000 CUSTOMERS $\times \$24.95 = \$24,950.00$

FIXED COST $- 8.00 = -8,000.00$ (EXAMPLE OFFICE EXPENSE)

MARKETING COST $-14.00 = -14,000.00$ (INCLUDES PRINTING, POSTAGE, LIST RENTAL, & LETTER SHOP)

MAILING PIECE -1.00 $-1,000.00$ (DIVIDE YOUR MAILING PIECE COST OF $5000 BY 5, 10, 20 OR AS MANY YEARS AS YOU PLAN TO USE IT).

TOTAL PROFIT $1.95 $1,950.00

As you can see, the total profit doesn't look real exciting. You will have to do one of three things to increase your profit line. As you begin to use this work sheet you may even uncover other ways to accomplish your goal. 1) raise your price of the product, 2) have a second item or another product to mail to your new customer, 3) lower your marketing costs. In direct marketing it's not often you break out (are in the black) on the first order. That's why you have to take your customer's profit line and see what he/she will spend with you over the next five years. This is also called a marketing history or lifetime history study. It is also called "what if!" After you have actual sales then go back and see how closely you were to your projections. Then the lifetime history study will complete the two parts—before and actual. Let's continue with our example.

The second year—or second mailing—you mail to your customer you will only need a letter, or a phone call to the customer to mail them another product. Immediately, your marketing cost all but vanished. We call one of these methods automatic or continuation shipments. Another marketing approach is the negative option. This marketing tool lets you mail a letter to your customer stating that if you don't hear from them in 10 days you will automatically send them the product. They have the option to keep the product or to send it back. In Chapter Twelve I will give you the exact rules for using this tool.

Now, let's see what happens to your customers over a five year period.

In my experience the continuation rate of sales ran about 60% of our original customers each year. Depending on the product it could go a bit higher or lower in sales. The graph below explains this pattern. The first year you had a response rate of .008 or 1000 customers.

FIRST YEAR	SECOND YEAR	THIRD YEAR	FOURTH YEAR	FIFTH YEAR
100%	60%	60%	60%	60%
1000	600	360	216	129

Now, let's take the second year or mailing and see how it functions.

GROSS SALE	$24.95 × 600 =	$14,970
FIXED COST	8.00 × 600 =	4,800
MARKETING	2.00 × 600 =	1,200
PROFIT	$14.95 × 600 =	$8,970

(Remember you have the customer. You may have a small cost)

Perhaps you are getting excited thinking you've made it. I'm afraid you still have lots of work to do. Over the first two years with your first marketing group you have made a profit total of $10,920. Continue working out all five years to see what your original year of marketing will bring you in profit and customers.

Don't forget that you will be doing new marketing each year—you divide all the received orders by the original fixed marketing cost of the mailing piece. Your fixed cost will come down each year or shipment, giving you more room for profit.

But you can't rest yet. The 125,000 test or first mailing is just the beginning. Perhaps the second marketing year you want to mail again. It is the general rule of thumb that 5 times your original mailing is safe. Personally, and several don't agree with me, I like to take 375,000 names to mail. This way if there are any mistakes, or you mail into the Superbowl, you won't sink. It is slower growing this way, but after all you aren't flush with money, are you? Now take the second mailing and track it just as you have the first. Remember, when you are going into a continuation mailing (renting more names from your test list) take only the lists that have functioned well for you. Say, you get a response on one of the lists of a .002 —don't do a continuation. If you get a response of .004 or better, then I'd say go ahead and rent additional sections of that list. This is not to say that you can't mail the .002 list again, it simply means that those orders will cost you more to get. The greater the list response the lower the cost to you.

HOW TO TRACK THE FIRST FIVE MAILINGS WITH CONTINUATION OF ORIGINAL CUSTOMERS: HORIZONTAL NUMBERS ARE EACH MAILING FROM ORIGINAL MAILING:

FIRST MAILING	1	2	3	4	5				
SECOND MAILING		1	2	3	4	5			
THIRD MAILING			1	2	3	4	5		
FOURTH MAILING				1	2	3	4	5	
FIFTH MAILING					1	2	3	4	5

ADD VERTICALLY for your net profit.

So many people only work out gross profit: I feel you should really plan net profit. This is really the bottom line. It may take you anywhere from three to five years to have a substantial net profit. Net profit is what you will take home. This is why, when starting out, you may need other means of support. You may only be mailing 10,000 names originally and so it will be slower going. But regardless of how many names you mail, the formula is the same.

On the third year (or third mailing) of the continuation mailing the formula is to mail again 5 times your continuation mailing. In the large numbers, I like to only mail 500,000 instead of $5 \times 375,000$. I guess I'm just more cautious. The main thing here is that you keep under control. If

18

you have mailed 10,000, now you could mail 50,000 advertising pieces; or you could mail 10,000 pieces again. And the bigger mailer can mail 375,000 pieces again, or go back to only 125,000 pieces. The important thing here is that you can work the formula to fit your budget, desire and time. You can work the numbers any way you want so it will work for you. Not everyone will be able to start out mailing 125,000 pieces of advertising. I only use that number as a starting place.

Example of
MATRIX FOR DETERMINING PRICE OF MAILING
PER THOUSAND
Based on 100,000 mailed
and $527.50 per thousand

(Fixed Cost)*

Component	Total Price	Per Thousand
Creative art package	$10,000	$100.00
Mechanicals	$ 7,339	$ 73.39

(Running Cost)*

List Mailing	$ 6,000	$ 60.00
Post Office 3rd class bulk rate	$12,500	$125.00
Printing (4 page letter, brochure order card, return envelope, outer envelope, guarantee card)	$31,604	$316.00
Lettershop	$ 2,650	$ 26.50
Total	$52,754	$527.50

*The creative $10,000 package and the mechanicals are a fixed cost and are not added into the mailing cost, the reason being that hopefully you will use the mailing package for many mailings: therefore the cost can be spread out over many years.

*Consider the other running costs that must be put against the actual mailing results each time you mail.

When you have finished this work sheet you can proudly take this to your banker. He will be so proud of you . . . and probably a bit surprised to see that it is possible to know what money you are going to need over the next five years. Good for you!

One of the most rewarding things a person can do before getting into his/her business is getting in touch with a business similar to the one you will be running. Oftentimes, by talking to them you can find out the inner secrets that will save you time and money. Inquire as to the return rate of a company's products, ask what suppliers the company uses, and so on. Examine the competition. See where you can do better—faster service, more cheerful approach, that sort of thing.

One more major thing we must cover while you are brainstorming your project is how you are going to mail the product. Your mailings will be going through the post office. So make a trip over to your friendly post office and meet the man in charge of the bulk mail division. The postman really likes to know his people. I can't say enough for the post office. They are outstanding and will do everything in their power to help you. When you approach the postmaster with what type of product you have in mind for mailing, the first thing he will do is try and determine what type of mailing permit you will need. He will fit you into one of the following classifications:

First class mail: All mailable matter may be sent as First Class Mail.

First class presort or bulk is defined as: Presort postage rates—you must have 500 pieces or more to qualify for a postage rate four cents per piece less than the regular letter rate. In addition to the four cents savings available for each piece of qualifying First-class mail sorted by zip code, the postal service offers a five cent discount for each piece. For example, there must be 10 or more pieces going to a specific carrier route to be eligible for the five cent discount. For more details send for the Domestic Mail Manual and look in Section 323.2. To qualify for bulk mailing, you must pay an annual fee of $60. The weight of the mailing piece cannot be more than 12 ounces each. Postage must be paid by postage meter stamps. And each envelope must be endorsed "Presorted First-class." Each mailing must be accompanied by a properly complete Form 3621—page 22.

First class mail may not be inspected by the post office. First class mail includes bills and statements, handwritten or typewritten matter, autograph albums containing writing, notebooks, printed forms filled out in writing, such as notices, certificates, checks cards or letters bearing a written date, and postal cards.

Second class mail consists of newspapers, circulars, magazines, and periodic publications. In other words, paper. The forms attached on page

Decisions! Decisions!

23 are self explanatory. Read over them a couple of times. Look over the form to see what is expected from you. The forms are very clear.

Second class takes a long time to get from the post office. Plan several months ahead in view of this time element.

Regular Third class description says it consists of advertising and printed promotional materials as well as parcels that weigh less than 16 ounces. It is not mailed or required to be mailed as First Class mail. Third Class bulk mail must consist of at least 200 pieces or 50 pounds. Each piece must be part of a group of 10 or more pieces sorted to the same carrier route, rural route, highway contract route, post office box section, etc. This class contains a wide range of items, from color catalogs to coupons. This class is used to inform, persuade, and convince someone they need the product. Regular 3rd class bulk mail permit takes only 3 days to receive. The postal service will require a sample of your mailing piece. If it fits all the specs, you're on your way. Each type of bulk mailing requires the payment of a flat rate at the beginning of each new year. In this section I have included forms that you will need to help figure out how your material should be classified. Take the book to the postal clerk and say, this is what I want. That way you'll be ahead of the game, and he will know you have done your homework.

The application for a special bulk third-class rate is shown on page 26.

Under the Third Class division is NONPROFIT ORGANIZATIONS ONLY. The non-profit groups really have a wonderful deal. If your product weighs under 16 ounces it can be mailed in bulk for around 25¢ each. Of course, if it weighs over that it will be priced differently. As you can imagine applying for eligibility to this division takes time. Your application has to have several o.k.'s and you have to prove you are nonprofit. Once your application goes through you'll be glad you made the effort.

Fourth Class division consists of mail not required to be mailed as First Class. Fourth Class weighs more than 16 ounces and it doesn't fit Second Class specs. These pieces are mailed at parcel post rates. You must mail 300 or more pieces. Parcels need not be identical size or weight. A telephone directory, for example, may be sent Fourth Class. This classification is bound printed matter that weighs at least one pound and not more than 10 pounds.

Perhaps you feel up to your eyes in details but this is the stuff that will not make you famous but will make you successful.

Presorted First Class Mail Form

<table>
<tr><td colspan="2">POSTMASTER: Remittance (payable to Postmaster) of annual mailing fee(s) for calendar year. (Check applicable box(es).)
NOTE: FEES are not refundable.</td><td>Year</td><td colspan="3">

(Name or mailer for whom bulk fee is paid—Print or Type above)</td></tr>
<tr><td>Presorted First-Class Mail, Carrier Route First-Class, and ZIP + 4 presort fee ($40 one fee for all)</td><td>Permit No.</td><td colspan="3">Address (Include ZIP Code)</td><td>Tel. No.</td></tr>
<tr><td>Presorted special Fourth-Class Mail fee ($40)</td><td>Permit No.</td><td colspan="4">Is name or address shown above different from that shown on reverse?</td></tr>
<tr><td>Third-Class Bulk mailing fee ($40)</td><td></td><td colspan="4" rowspan="2">☐ NO   ☐ YES (If YES, please advise)</td></tr>
<tr><td>Other</td><td></td></tr>
<tr><td>Meter License No.</td><td>Permit Imprint No.</td><td>Precanceled Stamps/Env Permit No.</td><td colspan="3">The letter shop, printing firm, or other organization shown below will act as our agent in preparing these mailings.

Mailing Agent (Name)</td></tr>
<tr><td colspan="3">NONPROFIT ORGANIZATIONS AUTHORIZED TO MAIL AT SPECIAL BULK RATES MUST COMPLETE THIS SECTION:</td><td colspan="2">Address (Include ZIP Code)</td><td>Tel. No.</td></tr>
<tr><td colspan="3">The purpose, function and nonprofit status of this organization and the exempt status for Federal income tax purposes (Check one)</td><td colspan="3"></td></tr>
<tr><td colspan="2">Changed during preceding 12 months?
(If "YES" submit written explanation of change with this form)</td><td>☐ YES

☐ NO</td><td colspan="2">Signature</td><td>Date</td></tr>
<tr><td colspan="3">Signature/Title</td><td colspan="3"></td></tr>
</table>

PS Form 3621, July 1984   MAILING FEE NOTICE

Second Class Sortation Instructions
AUTHORIZED PUBLICATIONS MAY BE ENDORSED "NEWSPAPER" OR 2C.

SORTATION REQUIREMENTS

BASIC SORTATION LEVELS

Packaging requirements:

Step 1 (5-digit packages)
Six or more pieces to same 5-digit zip code
Make into reasonable size packages
Apply red (D) label to top piece
Securely bind with rubber bands or string.

Step 2 (3-digit packages)
Six or more pieces to same 3-digit zip code
Make into reasonable size packages
Apply green (3) label to top piece
Securely bind with rubber bands, string, etc.

Step 3 (single-state packages)
Six or more pieces to same state
Make into reasonable size packages
Apply orange (S) label to top piece
Securely bind with rubber bands, string, etc.

Step 4 (mixed state packages)
Package remaining residue
Place "Mixed States" label on top.

22

U.S. Postal Service   STATEMENT OF MAILING—2nd CLASS PUBS EXCEPT REQUESTER PUBLICATIONS (See DMM 482)   **Side A**

Name of Publication or News Agent		Publication No.	Date of Mailing
			(Mo.) (Day) (Yr.)

Post Office and State of Mailing	ZIP Code	Finance Number	Frequency of issue	Date of issue printed in copies

Statement No. *(In sequence)*	To be completed for each mailing of each issue unless mailer is authorized to submit one statement for all issues *(see DMM 482)*	When this statement is for ALL ISSUES for a calendar month, show total pounds in items 1 and 12. In order to compute per piece charges, multiply the number of addressed pieces per issue by the number of issues and put the result in the appropriate blocks of items 5, 9, 10, 13, and 14. Also furnish the following information:
Freight Bill No.		Number of issues this month
Edition Code or Key	Average weight per copy for the issue *(see DMM 482.23)* _____ . _____ LBS.	Weight of one sheet *(see DMM 482.34)* _____ . _____ LBS.
Check if incidental First-Class enclosed ☐	Percent of advertising ➤ _____ %	Combined weight of one copy from each issue _____ . _____ LBS.
	Post Office computed average or combined weight per copy _____ LBS.	Percent of advertising in total month's issues _____ %

When postage is computed at the key rate, the lines for Zones 1 to 8 need not be completed for each issue. The total zone mailings must be entered in Item 1 during the time the key rate is in effect.

1.		Zone	A *Non-subscriber's Copies	B Subscriber's Copies	C Total Copies	D Total *(Pounds)*	E Advertising Portion *(Pounds)*	F. Postage Rate Per Pound or Fraction — Regular		G Computed Postage
		AND 2						$0.165		
	Check if Science of Agriculture Publication	3						$0.174		
		4						$0.191		
		5						$0.216		
		6						$0.243		
		7						$0.275		
		8						$0.302		
	TOTAL COPIES							Total advertising postage		

OUTSIDE COUNTY / POUND RATE

2. TOTAL POUNDS ALL ZONES

3. Total advertising portion *(Col. E line 2)*   ▲ Key rate, if used ▲

4. Nonadvertising Portion *(Col. D line 2 minus line 3)* $0.124

5. For mailing of copies to destinations outside county of publication

LEVEL	A. Copies not meeting requirements for level B or C rate.	Total Copies	No. of Addressed Pieces	$0.160	Postage
	B. Packages of six or more addressed pieces labeled and sacked to 5-digit, 3-digit city or optional city destinations (see DMM 468)	Total Copies	No. of Addressed Pieces	$0.124	Postage
	C. Packages of six or more addressed pieces labeled and sacked to carrier route or carrier routes destinations (see DMM 468)	Total Copies	No. of Addressed Pieces	$0.099	Postage
	D. Subtotal (5A, B, and C) ➤				

PER PIECE RATES *(in addition to the pound rate)*

9A. Nonadvertising Portion (See DMM 411.25 or 411.355)
Nonadv. Percentage (Divide by 100, e.g., 49.05 ÷ 100 = .4905) _____ × .04 = Nonadv. Factor (Round up to four decimal places, e.g., .01962 = .0197) _____ × No. of addressed Pieces in line 5. _____ = $ _____   Postage Reduction

9B. TOTAL Piece Charge *(5D minus 9A)* ➤

10. Intra SCF Rate—This rate can only be claimed for pieces for delivery within the SCF of Mailing. Pieces paid for at in-county rates are not eligible for this rate. (see DMM 468)   Postage Reduction

Three-digit ZIP Codes within SCF of Mailing _____ . Intra SCF Rate

Number of qualifying pieces in item 5 _____ × $0.010 = $ _____

11. TOTAL outside county piece charge (Item 9B minus Item 10) ➤

IN-COUNTY

12. POUND RATE	Nonsubscriber Copies	Subscriber Copies	**Total Copies**	Total Pounds	$0.094

13. PER PIECE CHARGES *(In addition to the pound rate.)*

LEVEL	J. Copies not meeting requirements for level K rate (see DMM 468)	Total Copies	No. of Addressed Pieces	$0.057
	K. Packages of six or more addressed pieces labeled and sacked to carrier route or carrier routes destinations (see DMM 468)	Total Copies	No. of Addressed Pieces	$0.032

14. FOREIGN (Publishers Periodicals) (see IMM 242.2) WEIGHT PER COPY *(must include the wrapping)*	Nonsubscriber Copies	Subscriber Copies	Total Copies	Rate Per Copy

15. NONSUBSCRIBER COPIES
Complete Form 3541-A for commingled nonsubscriber copies which exceed the 10% allowance in DMM 411.322 & 411.4 and attach to this Form.   Compute postage on attached Form 3541-A and write postage amount in Col. G of this line for nonsubscriber copies in excess of 10% limit. ➤

I hereby certify that all information furnished on this form is accurate and truthful, and that this material presented qualifies for the rates of postage claimed.

16. MAILED BY *(Signature required)*	18. COMPUTED BY *(Signature required)*	
17. TELEPHONE NO.		**TOTAL POSTAGE** ➤

The submission of a false, fictitious or fraudulent statement may result in imprisonment of up to 5 years and a fine of up to $10,000. (18 U.S.C. 1001) In addition, a civil penalty of up to $5,000 and an additional assessment of twice the amount falsely claimed may be imposed. (31 U.S.C. 3802)

* Only nonsubscriber copies within the 10% limitation are to be shown in items 1 thru 14 of this Form. Postage for commingled nonsubscriber copies that exceed the 10% limit is to be reported on Form 3541-A. Nonsubscriber copies in excess of the 10% limit in 411.322 & 411.4 which are not commingled with subscriber copies are not mailable at second-class rates. **(Mailer must fill in unshaded blocks.)**

PS Form 3541, Apr. 1988   FINANCIAL DOCUMENT — FORWARD TO FINANCE OFFICER

MANDATORY SECOND-CLASS MAIL PREPARATION REQUIREMENTS

Pieces qualifying for the rate MUST be prepared in the following sequence:

Firm	5-Digit	3-Digit	State	Mixed States

5-Digit

Philadelphia PA 19118
2C
Boston MA 021

Six or more pieces for the same 5 digits must be packaged and sacked in the following priority order:

5-digit sack. When the first 5 digits are the same.

3-digit sack. When the first 3 digits are the same.

State sack. When the addresses are for the same State.

Mixed states sack.

3-Digit

Philadelphia PA 191
2C
Boston MA 021

Six or more pieces for the same first 3 digits when not sufficient to make a 5-digit package are to be packaged and sacked in the following priority order:

3-digit sack. When the first 3 digits are the same.

State sack. When the addresses are for the same State.

Mixed states sack.

State

DIS Kansas City MO 640
2C MO
San Francisco CA 941

Six or more pieces for a State when not sufficient to make a 3-digit package must be packaged and sacked in the following priority order:

State sack. When the addresses are for the same State.

Mixed states sack.

Mixed States

DIS Chicago IL 606
2C   Mixed States
Chicago IL 606

Remaining pieces are to be packaged and placed in a mixed states sack.

Firm

Copies for which one piece charge is paid must be packaged and sacked in the following priority order:

5-digit sack. When the first 5 digits are the same.

3-digit sack. When the first 3 digits are the same.

State sack. When the addresses are for the same state.

Mixed states sack.

*Note: Exception:, "Loose Packing" of pieces in full No. 3 sacks may be authorized by MSC managers (for 5 digits only).

Note: Only required sortations are depicted. There are several optional sorts which will, in many cases, result in improved service. Mailers are encouraged to make these additional sorts, which are described in Chapter 4 of the Domestic Mail Manual, particularly for their local areas.

24

APPLICATION TO MAIL AT SPECIAL BULK THIRD-CLASS RATES

PART 1 - FOR COMPLETION BY APPLICANT	SECTION A - APPLICATION

NOTE: PLEASE READ ALL INFORMATION IN SECTION B ON THE BACK OF THIS APPLICATION BEFORE COMPLETING THE FORM BELOW.

Instructions

A. Be sure that all information entered below is legible so that our records will show the correct information about your organization

B. Show the complete name of the organization in item 1. The name shown must agree with the name that appears on all documents submitted to support this application.

C. A complete address representing a physical location for the organization must be shown in item 2. When mail is received through a post office box, show your street address first and then the box number.

D. The name of the applicant in item 5 must be the name of the individual submitting the application for the organization. The individual must be an officer of the organization. Printers and mailing agents may not sign for the organization.

E. No additional categories may be added in item 6. You must qualify as one of the types of organizations listed in order to be eligible for special rates.

F. Be sure to sign the application in item 12.

G. The date shown in item 14 must be the date that you submit the application to the post office.

NO APPLICATION FEE IS REQUIRED

Please be sure all information is complete.	PLEASE TYPE OR PRINT LEGIBLY

1. Complete Name of Organization

2. Address of Organization (Street, Apt./ Suite No.)

3. City, State, ZIP+4 Code

4. (Area Code)/ Telephone No.

( )

5. Name of Applicant (must represent organization that is applying.)

6. Type of Organization (Check only one. See 'E' above.)

☐ (01) Religious ☐ (03) Scientific ☐ (05) Agricultural ☐ (07) Veterans ☐ (09) Qualified Political Committee

☐ (02) Educational ☐ (04) Philanthropic ☐ (06) Labor ☐ (08) Fraternal

7. Check whether this organization is for profit or whether any of the net income inures to the benefit of any private stockholder or individual.

☐ YES ☐ NO

8. Check whether this organization is exempt from Federal income tax. (If 'YES', attach a copy of the exemption issued by the Internal Revenue Service which shows the section of the IRS code under which the organization is exempt. If an application for exempt status is pending with the IRS, you must check the 'NO' box.)

☐ YES ☐ NO

9. POST OFFICE where authorization is requested and bulk mailings will be made (City, State, and ZIP+4 Code of Main Post Office)
NOTE: An authorization may NOT be requested at a station or branch of a post office.

10. If your organization has previously mailed at the special bulk rates, list the post offices where mailings were most recently deposited at these rates:

11. Has your organization had special bulk third-class rate mailing privileges denied or revoked? If you answered "YES", please list the post office (City and State) where an application was denied or an authorization was revoked:

☐ YES

☐ NO

I certify that the statements made by me are true and complete. I understand that if this application for authorization is approved, it may only be used for our organization's mail at the post office specified above, and that we may not transfer or extend it to any other mailer. I further understand that if this application is approved, a postage refund for the difference between the regular and special bulk rates may be made for only those regular bulk third-class mailings entered at the post office identified above during the period this application is pending, provided the conditions set forth in section 642.4, Domestic Mail Manual, are met.

12. SIGNATURE OF APPLICANT

13. TITLE

14. DATE

Willful entry or submission of false, fictitious or fraudulent statements or representations in this application may result in a fine up to $10,000 or imprisonment up to 5 years or both (18 U.S.C.1001)

PART 2 - POSTMASTER AT ORIGINATING OFFICE
This part should be completed at the time the application is filed with your office

1. Signature of Postmaster (or designated representative)

2. Date application was filed with your office (Round Stamp)

PS Form 3624, April 1987   (Page 1 of 3)

CHECK LIST TO REVIEW COMPLETENESS OF PS FORM 3624 AND SUPPORTING DOCUMENTATION

PART A: FORM COMPLETION

1. _____ Name of organization requesting special third-class mailing privileges.

2. _____Telephone number of organization.

3. _____Street address of organization.

4. _____City, state and zip + 4 code of organization.

5. _____City, state, and zip + 4 code of post office of mailing.

6. _____Type of organization requesting special mailing privileges. (Only one type accepted & no additions accepted)

7. _____Must be completed.

8. _____Must be completed. If "yes" is checked, the Internal Revenue Service letter must be attached.

9. _____Signature of an officer in applicant organization. (Signature of mailing agent not acceptable.)

10. _____Title of officer signing.

11. _____Date application submitted.
12 thru 14.—Completed by the Rates and Classification Center (RCC).

PART B: SUPPORTING DOCUMENTATION REQUIRED

1. _____Proof of Nonprofit status
Examples of Acceptable Evidence:
—Current Internal Revenue Service letter of tax exemption under Section 501C of the Internal Revenue Code
—Current copy of financial statement conducted by an independent auditor or CPA

2. _____Proof of how the organization is organized
Examples of Acceptable Evidence:
—Current charter
—Current articles of incorporation
—Current constitution and bylaws

3. _____Proof of how the organization is operated
Examples of Acceptable Evidence:
—Most recent newsletters, bulletins, brochures, etc.
—Schedule or listing of activities for past 12 months
—Minutes of meetings held in past 12 months

Signature of Employee Completing Check List Date of Completion Phone Number

When you receive your mailing permit you will then need an "indicia".

Sample of Indicia

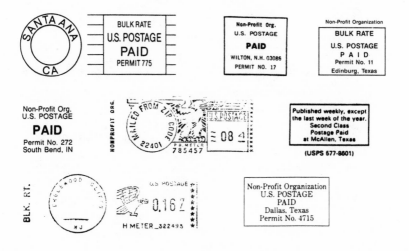

27

BASIC RATE
REQUIRED PACKAGING
"RULE OF TEN"

- 5-Digit   "Ten" or more pieces to one 5-digit zip code
- 3-Digit   "Ten" or more pieces to the same first 3-digit zip code remaining after all 5-digit packages are prepared
- State   "Ten" or more pieces to one state remaining after all 5-digit and 3-digit packages are prepared
- MXD States   All remaining pieces that do not make up any States category above.

Labeling Packages of Mail
with Pressure Sensitive Labels

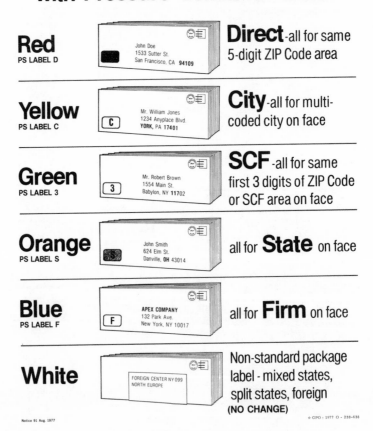

Red
PS LABEL D

John Doe
1533 Sutter St.
San Francisco, CA **94109**

Direct-all for same 5-digit ZIP Code area

Yellow
PS LABEL C

C

Mr. William Jones
1234 Anyplace Blvd.
YORK, PA **17401**

City-all for multi-coded city on face

Green
PS LABEL 3

3

Mr. Robert Brown
1554 Main St.
Babylon, NY **11702**

SCF-all for same first 3 digits of ZIP Code or SCF area on face

---

Orange
PS LABEL S

John Smith
624 Elm St.
Danville, **OH** 43014

all for **State** on face

Blue
PS LABEL F

F

APEX COMPANY
132 Park Ave.
New York, NY 10017

all for **Firm** on face

White

FOREIGN CENTER NY 099
NORTH EUROPE

Non-standard package label - mixed states, split states, foreign
(NO CHANGE)

Notice 91 Aug. 1977

e GPO : 1977 O - 238-636

28

INFORMATION ON BULK 3RD CLASS, PERMITS, RESTRICTIONS, AND PREPARATION OF MAIL

Bulk Rate—3rd Class (Under 16 ozs. and not first class matter)

A. Payment of Postage can be by:
   1. Meter
   2. Permit Imprint
   3. Precancelled Stamps

B. Fees—
   Application Fee (Form 3601)—$60.00 (one time)
   Yearly Calendar Fee—$60.00

C. Rates—
   See Attached Rates

D. Markings Required—
   1. Bulk rate or the abbreviation Blk. Rt., or NonProfit Organization or abbreviation NonProfit Org., Permit No. must be printed or rubber stamped by the mailer either in or adjacent to permit imprints, meter stamps or precancelled stamps.

E. Minimum Mailings at a Time—200 pieces or 50 pounds.

F. Mailing—
   1. Must be presented at the Main Post Office, 620 E. Pecan.
   2. Form 3624 in duplicate, properly completed, must accompany each mailing. (3624PC for mailings using precancelled stamps)
   3. Sufficient funds must be deposited on account to cover cost of entire mailing.

G. Weight and Size Limits—
   1. No maximum size.
   2. Must not be less than 3½ inches in width (height) or 5 inches in length.
   3. Only rectangular pieces are mailable.
   4. Ratio of width (height) to length, between 1 to 1.3 and 1 to 2.5.
   5. Cards must have a thickness of at least .007 inches.

H. Mail Preparation
   1. Makeup
      All pieces must be faced in one way with a plainly addressed piece, including Zip Code, on top.
      (1) Five digit package—Place 10 or more pieces for same Zip Code area in bundle—Affix Red Label D.
      (2) Mixed City Package—Place 10 or more pieces bearing more than one Zip Code but addressed to Multi-coded city in bundle—Affix Yellow Label C.
      (3) Sectional Center Packages—Place 10 or more pieces for more than one post office in the same SCF (first 3 digits of Zip Code) in a bundle. Affix Green Label 3.
      (4) State Packages—After 5 digit, mixed city and SCF packages have been made, place 10 or more pieces remaining for the same state in bundle. Affix Orange Label S.
      (5) Mixed City Package, Sectional Center Package and State Packages are also referred to as *Basic*.
   2. Affixing Labels
      (1) Pressure sensitive labels on the lower left-hand corner of the face of the top piece on letter-size packages. On flats, apply pressure sensitive label adjacent to the address on the top mail piece.
      (2) Use non-standard package labels only when a coded pressure sensitive label cannot be used. Non-standard labels are used to identify mixed states, split states, and foreign packages. This label when fixed should cover the entire address portion of the top mail piece.
   3. Listing Required.
      (1) When a third-class 5-digit presort level rate mailing consists of pieces to be mailed at the basic rate, the mailer is required to provide the post office with a list of the number of qualifying pieces to each ZIP Code destination except as noted in 622.12c(2).
      (2) A list of the number of qualifying pieces being mailed to each ZIP code destination is not required when all sacks containing identical weight third-class 5-digit presort

level rate pieces are physically separated at the time of mailing from all sacks containing identical weight pieces to be mailed at the basic rate.
4. Packages
    (1) When 10 or more individually addressed pieces to the destination, as in H above, they must be *securely wrapped or tied together*. It is the responsibility of the mailer to properly prepare and present mailings. Remember that the reduced rate is made available *only* because the properly prepared mailing reduces work necessary within the Post Office.

NOTE: Foreign mail cannot be mailed with a domestic mail mailing. Contact the Post Office regarding rates and preparation.

U.S. POSTAL SERVICE

Dear Postal Customer:

Bulk Third-Class Sacking Requirements Have Changed!!!!

On August 24, 1986, a new set of minimum sacking requirements became mandatory for all bulk third-class mailers. A major benefit of the new regulations is that they will generally reduce the number of sacks that you will have to prepare and help relieve the periodic sack sorting capacity problems at many of our Bulk Mail Centers (BMC's).

Under the Postal Service's bulk mail verification procedures, when a mailing is verified and determined to have 10 percent or more errors in presort and mail make-up, you would normally be given the option of either reworking the mailing so it does qualify for the bulk rate of postage or paying the single piece rate on the portion of the entire mailing estimated to be in error.

However, through September 30, 1986, bulk third-class mailings which did not meet the 125 piece/15 pound minimum requirements under the following condition were accepted. The present requirements are as follows:

1. All mailings must be prepared in accordance with all preparation requirements (i.e., package preparation and labeling, sack labeling, etc.), except for the 125 piece/15 pound minimum sack requirement.

2. If a mailing is found to contain 10 percent or more error in presort and mail make-up, excluding the minimum sacking requirement, there are two options:

    a. Pay the single piece rate on the percentage of the mailing estimated to be in error, OR

    b. Rework the mailing to correct noted errors and also to meet the 125 piece/15 pound minimum sacking requirements so that it qualifies for the bulk rate of postage.

Mailings which do not meet the minimum sacking requirements will not be accepted and no further exceptions will be granted.

We appreciate your cooperation in this matter. I have attached a copy of the new bulk third-class minimum sacking requirements for your information. If you have any questions regarding the new requirements or the options explained above, you should contact Bulk Mail Section for assistance.

NEW BULK THIRD-CLASS SACKING REQUIREMENTS

Effective April 20, 1986, Domestic Mail Manual (DMM) 622 and 667 are revised to incorporate a new set of sacking requirements for bulk third-class mail. These new sacking requirements are designed to eliminate mailers' preparation of lightweight sacks of bulk third-class mail which over the years have created inefficiencies in postal operations.

Summary of Changes

In general, the new regulations will increase the minimum sacking requirements for most sacks of bulk third-class mail from current levels to 125 pieces or 15 pounds of mail. Also, under the new regulations, carrier route and 5-digit mail will qualify for the discounted rates when sacked to 3-digit destinations. These changes affect only bulk third-class sacking requirements. The minimum quantity required per mailing remains unchanged at 200 pieces or 50 pounds of mail. Similarly, packaging requirements are unchanged.

Third-Class Sacks Survey

The new regulations are based upon a survey of third-class sacks and a study which analyzed the current minimum sacking requirements for bulk third-class mail. The sacking survey was undertaken to determine the characteristics of current bulk third-class sacks. The results of this survey showed that lightweight sacks of bulk third-class mail make up a substantial portion of our sack handling workloads.

The minimum sacking study was designed to examine our current sacking requirements to determine a more economical set of sacking requirement for bulk third-class mail which, in turn, would lower operating costs and help relieve sack sorting capacity problems at bulk mail centers (BMCs) and other facilities. The results of this study indicated that the current minimum sacking requirements for bulk third-class mail are significantly below the levels that were determined to be the most economical. The new sacking requirements, presented below, are based on the results of this study.

As noted above, the new regulations will produce lower operating costs and help to relieve the strain on BMC sack sorting capacities. They should also provide benefits for mailers. The new regulations will reduce the number of sacks prepared by mailers, and this should result in lower preparation costs for mailers. Also, the reduction in required sack preparations will lower sack demand providing relief from sack shortages experienced by many mailers.

Chapter 3—Third-Class Mail

622 Third-Class Bulk Mail
622.1 Eligibility

.11 Carrier Route Presort Level

a. Minimum Quantity. Each mailing must consist of at least 200 pieces or 50 pounds of mail presorted to carrier routes in accordance with 667.3. Each piece must be part of a group of 10 or more pieces packaged to the same carrier route, rural route, highway contract route, post office box section, or general delivery unit. Packages must be placed in either a carrier route, 5-digit carrier routes, or 3-digit carrier routes sack. Each sack must contain a minimum of 125 pieces or 15 pounds of qualifying carrier route packages to be eligible for the carrier route presort level rate.

b. Residual. Those pieces not part of a group of 10 or more pieces packaged to a particular carrier route, or those which are part of a group of 10 or more pieced packaged to a particular carrier route but which cannot be placed in sack containing a minimum of 125 pieces or 15 pounds of qualifying mail, are residual pieces. Residual pieces may be included in a carrier route presort rate mailing and may bear the Carrier Route Presort endorsement subject to the following provisions:

(1) Residual pieces do not count towards the minimum quantity requirements for the carrier route presort level rate.

(2) The number of residual pieces to any single 5-digit ZIP Code area may not exceed 5 percent of the total qualifying presorted carrier route pieces addressed to that 5-digit area.

(3) Residual pieces are not eligible for the carrier route presort level rate and must have postage paid at the appropriate third-class "basic" level bulk rate.

(4) Residual pieces must be prepared in accordance with 667.3.

622.12 Five-Digit Presort Level

.12 Five-Digit Presort Level

a. Minimum Quantity. Each mailing must consist of at least 200 pieces or 50 pounds of qualifying mail presorted to 5-digit destinations. Each piece must be part of a package of 10 or more pieces to the same 5-digit ZIP Code destination and the packages must be placed in a 5-digit, unique 3-digit city or 3-digit sack as follows:

(1) Five-digit sacks must contain a minimum of 125 pieces or 15 pounds of mail.

Exception: Five-digit sacks containing 10 or more pounds of mail which are part of a machinable parcel mailing prepared in accordance with 667.2, will qualify for the 5-digit presort rate level.

(2) For unique 3-digit multi-ZIP Code cities listed in Exhibit 122.63B, mailers may commingle different 5-digit packages of 10 or more pieces in unique 3-digit city sacks providing:

(a) Each sack contains at least 125 pieces or 15 pounds of mail, and

(b) Three-digit city packages are NOT included in the sack, and

(c) 125 pieces or 15 pounds of mail for a single 5-digit ZIP Code (within the unique 3-digit city) must be sacked separately.

(3) Three-digit sacks must contain a minimum of 125 pieces or 15 pounds of mail with a minimum of 50 pieces or 10 pounds to each 5-digit ZIP Code destination contained within the 3-digit sack.

Note—Sacks containing fewer than 125 pieces or less than 15 pounds of mail will NOT be accepted. Fifty pieces or 10 pounds of mail for a 5-digit destination will qualify for the 5-digit presort level rate when prepared in packages and bundles presented on pallets in accordance with 667.

667.1 Preparation Requirements for Basic Rate

.13 Sacking Requirements
.131 General

a. Sack Preparation. Packages must be sorted and sacked to destinations in accordance with 667.132a through 667.132h. Mailers must note on the mailing statement submitted with the mailing whether the 125 piece or 15 pound minimum, or both, were used as the basis for preparing the entire mailing in sacks.

Exceptions:

(1) If authorized to bundle or palletize, mailers must prepare packages and bundles in accordance with 667.5 or 667.6.

(2) Mailers who Express Mail drop ship bulk third-class mailings in accordance with 136.7 may prepare sack containing fewer than 125 pieces or less than 15 pounds of mail.

b. Sack Label Color. Sack labels must be white or manila (other colors will not be accepted).

c. Sack Weight. No more than 70 pounds of mail may be placed in any sack.

.132 Sortation

a. 5-Digit Sacks. When there are 125 pieces or 15 pounds of mail packaged to the same 5-digit ZIP Code destination, the packages MUST be placed in a 5-digit sack labeled to the 5-digit destination. Five-digit sacks containing fewer than 125 pieces or less than 15 pounds of mail will NOT be accepted. Each sack must be labeled in the following manner:

Line 1:   City, State and 5-digit destination
Line 2:   Contents.
Line 3:   Office of Mailing.
Sample: PHILADELPHIA PA 19118
          3C FLATS
          BOSTON MA

Note: If a mailing consists of both machinable parcel and irregular parcels as defined in 128 and as provided for in 622.14, the contents line of 5-digit sack labels must read "3C MACH and IRREG." When there are 10 pounds of material for a 5-digit ZIP Code destination, it must be placed in a 5-digit sack. Sacks containing less than 10 pounds of mail may be prepared. Pieces in a 5-digit sack that contains machinable and irregular parcels need not be packaged as required by 677.121b.

b. Optional City Sacks. If after preparing required 5-digit sacks, there are 125 pieces or 15 pounds of mail packaged to the multi-ZIP Coded cities listed in Exhibit 122.63a, mailers are encouraged to place those packages into city sacks. City sacks containing fewer than 15 pieces or less than 15 pounds will NOT be accepted. Each sack must be labeled in the following manner:

Line 1:   City, State and Lowest 5-digit ZIP Code.
Line 2:   Contents.
Line 3:   Office of Mailing.
Sample: AURORA IL 60504
          3C LTRS
          BOSTON MA

Note: An optional city sack may contain both machinable and irregular parcels (as defined in 128) when there are at least 10 pounds of material for the optional city sack. The contents line for optional city sack labels for sacks which are part of a mailing containing machinable and irregular parcels must read "3C MACH AND IRREG." Pieces in an optional city sack that contains both machinable and irregular parcels need not be packaged as required by 667.121c.

c. 3-Digit Sacks. When after preparing required 5-digit and optional city sacks, there are 125 pieces or 15 pounds of mail packaged to the same 3-digit ZIP Code destination, the packages MUST be placed in a 3-digit sack labeled to the 3-digit destination. Three-digit sacks containing fewer than 125 pieces or less than 15 pounds of mail will NOT be accepted. Each sack must be labeled in the following manner:

Line 1:   City, State and 3-digit ZIP Code prefix.
Line 2:   Contents.
Line 3:   Office of Mailing.
Sample: PHILADELPHIA PA 191
          3C FLTS
          ROCHESTER NY

d. Optional SCF Sacks. When, after preparing required 5-digit, optional city, and required 3-digit sacks, there are 125 pieces or 15 pounds of mail packaged to post offices in the same sectional center facility (SCF) service areas listed in 122.63d, mailers are encouraged to place the packages into SCF sacks. SCF sacks containing fewer than 125 pieces or less than 15 pounds of mail will NOT be accepted. Each sack must be labeled in the following manner:

Line 1:   Name and State of SCF and Lowest 3-digit ZIP Code for that SCF.
Line 2:   Contents.
Line 3:   Office of Mailing.
Sample: SCF PHILADELPHIA PA 190
          3C FLATS
          BOSTON MA

Note: A list of all SCFs serving more than one 3-digit ZIP Code area, the first three digits of all ZIP Codes served by these facilities, and the principal 3-digit ZIP Code prefix that is to be used on SCF sack labels is contained in Exhibit 122.63d.

e. Optional SDC Sacks. When, after preparing required 5-digit, optional city, required 3-digit and optional SCF sacks, there are 125 pieces or 15 pounds of mail addressed to post offices in the same state distribution center (SDC) service areas listed in Exhibits 122.63g and 122.63h, mailers are encouraged to prepare SDC sacks. SDC sacks contained fewer than 125 pieces or less than 15 pounds ill NOT be accepted. Each sack must be labeled in the following manner:

Line 1: Name and 2-Letter State
Abbreviation of SDC for Destination Area and ZIP Code (3-digit or 5-digit as appropriate).
Line 2: Contents and 2-Letter State Abbreviation.
Line 3: Office of Mailing.
Sample: DIS PITTSBURGH PA 150
3C FLTS PA
SAN FRANCISCO CA

f. State Sacks. When, after preparing required 5-digit, optional city, required 3-digit optional SCF, and optional SDC sacks, there are 125 pieces or 15 pounds of mail packaged to the same state, the packages MUST be placed into state sacks. Sacks containing fewer than 125 pieces or less than 15 pounds may be prepared. Each sack must be labeled in accordance with Exhibits 122.63j, 122.63k, or 122.63l, as applicable, and in the following manner:

Line 1: Name and 2-Letter State
Abbreviation of SDC for State of Destination and XIP Code (3-digit or 5-digit as appropriate).
Line 2: Contents and 2-Letter State Abbreviation.
Line 3: Office of Mailing.
Sample: DIS KANSAS CITY MO 640
3C LTRS MO
SCRANTON PA

g. Mixed States Sacks. If after all required and optional sacks have been prepared, there are packages remaining for more than one state, the mail must be placed into MIXED STATES sacks. Each MIXED STATES sack must be labeled in the following manner:

Line 1: Mixed States Distribution Location.
Line 2: Contents followed by the words "MIXED STATES"
Line 3: Office of Mailing.
Sample: DIS CHICAGO IL 606
3C LTRS MXD STATES
CHICAGO IL

Note: The last sack in a mailing may not necessarily be a MIXED STATES sack. For example, if there are 10 pieces remaining for a 3-digit ZIP Code area, which could not be placed in any of the required or optional sacks prepared, those pieces must be placed in a sack and labeled to the 3-digit ZIP Code destination. Equally, the last sack of a mailing could be for any level of sortation and is dependent upon the mail remaining after all required and optional sacks have been prepared. The last sack must be labeled to the appropriate destination depending on the mail for which the sack was prepared.

h. Loose Pack Sack. The term "loose pack sack" refers to the placement of unpackaged, unbound mail pieces in a receptacle such as a mail sack. Management Sectional Center (MSC) managers may authorize mailers to loose pack pieces in full No. 3 sacks without packaging when all material in a sack would normally be "worked" at the point where the sack is opened, e.g., if a 3-digit sack contains no more than nine pieces for any one 5-digit destination. Pieces must be placed to maintain orientation of the pieces while in transit. Mailers desiring to loose pack pieces must be request authorization through the post office of mailing.

Note: The following abbreviations may be used on the contents line of sack and pallet labels for basic rate level mailings:

34

```
LETTERS . . . . . . . . . . . . . . . . . . . . . . . . . . . . . . . . . . . . . . . . . . . . . . . . . .LTRS
FLATS. . . . . . . . . . . . . . . . . . . . . . . . . . . . . . . . . . . . . . . . . . . . . . . . . . .FLTS
MIXED . . . . . . . . . . . . . . . . . . . . . . . . . . . . . . . . . . . . . . . . . . . . . . . . . .MXD
DIGIT . . . . . . . . . . . . . . . . . . . . . . . . . . . . . . . . . . . . . . . . . . . . . . . . . . .DG
```

667.2 Machinable Parcel Preparation Requirements

.22 Sacking Requirement

.221 5-Digit Sacks. When there are 10 or more pounds of mail addressed to the same 5-digit ZIP Code destination, it may be placed in 5-digit sacks. Sacks containing less than 10 pounds of mail will NOT be accepted. Each sack must be labeled in the following manner:

Line 1: City, State and 5-digit Destination.
Line 2: Contents.
Line 3: Office of Mailing.
Sample: BINGHAMTON NY 13901
               3C MACH
               WASHINGTON DC

.222 Destination Bulk Mail Center (BMC) Sacks. If, after preparing 5-digit sacks there are 10 pounds or more of mail to a destination BMC delivery area, it must be placed in a destination BMC sack. Each sack must be labeled in the following manner:

Line 1: Destination BMC and 2-Letter State Abbreviation and Zip Code.
Line 2: Contents.
Line 3: Office of Mailing.
Sample: BM CHICAGO IL 608
               3C MACH
               ATLANTA GA

667.3 Preparation Requirements for Carrier Route Presort Level Rate

.31 Packaging

.312 Residual Packages. All residual packages MUST be labeled with a RED label "D" to facilitate postal verification and handling and be placed in 3-digit carrier routes sacks. Residual packages MUST be prepared in one of the following ways:

a. Residual packages of 10 or more pieces to the same carrier (those which could not be placed in a sack containing at least 125 pieces or 15 pounds of mail) must be labeled with a Red Label "D" and placed in a 3-digit carrier routes sack. In addition to the Red Label "D", residual carrier packages may also be labeled to the carrier route in accordance with 667.311 a or b.

b. Residual pieces of fewer than 10 pieces to a single carrier route may be secured in packages in accordance with 667.311. In addition to the Red Label "D" residual carrier packages may also be labeled to the carrier route in accordance with 667.311 a or b.

c. Residual pieces for an individual carrier route not packaged to a carrier route as provided in 667.312a or 667.312b, must be made up into 5-digit packages.

.321 Sacking

General.

a. Sack Preparation. All qualifying packages of 10 or more pieces to the same carrier route must be placed in sacks in accordance with 667.322 through 667.324. Mailers must note on the mailing statement submitted with the mailing whether the 125 piece or 15 pound minimum, or both, were used as the basis for preparing the entire mailing in sacks.

Exceptions:

(1) If authorized to bundle or palletize, mailers must prepare packages and bundles in accordance with 667.5 or 667.6.

(2) Mailers who Express Mail drop ship bulk third-class mailings in accordance with 136.7 may prepare sacks containing fewer than 125 pieces or less than 15 pounds of mail.

b. Sack Label Color. Sack labels must be white or manila (other colors will not be accepted).

c. Sack Weight. No more than 70 pounds of mail may be placed in any sack.

.322 Carrier Route Sacks. When there are 125 pieces or 15 pounds of qualifying mail to the same carrier route the mail should be placed in a Carrier Route sack. Carrier Route sacks containing fewer than 125 pieces or less than 15 pounds of mail for the same carrier route will NOT be accepted. Each sack must be labeled in the following manner:

Line 1: City, State and 5-Digit ZIP Code Destination.
Line 2: Contents and Carrier Route, Rural Route, Post Office Box Section, Highway Contract Route, or General Delivery Unit.
Line 3: Office of Mailing.
Sample: SAN FRANCISCO CA 94133
3C LTRS—CR 18
PORTLAND OR

.323 Five-Digit Carrier Routes Sacks. When, after preparing all Carrier Route sacks, there are 125 pieces or 15 pounds of qualifying mail to different carrier routes within the same 5-digit ZIP Code area the mail must be laced in 5-digit Carrier Routes sacs labeled to the 5-digit ZIP Code destination. Five-Digit Carrier Routes sacks containing fewer than 125 pieces or less than 15 pounds of mail may only be prepared under the following exception:

Exceptions: Saturation mailers of carrier route presorted mail may, at their option, prepare 5-digit Carrier Routes sacks containing fewer than 125 pieces or less than 15 pounds of mail for those 5-digit ZIP Code areas that do not have a sufficient number of residentail deliveries to meet the 125 piece minimum at a 90 percent saturation level. A saturation mailing is defined as a mailing sent to at least 90 percent of the total residential addresses within a 5-digit ZIP Code area. Five-Digit Carrier Routes sacks must be labeled in the following manner:

Line 1: City, State and 5-digit ZIP Code Destination.
Line 2: Contents followed by the words CARRIER ROUTES.
Line 3: Office of Mailing.
Sample: SAN FRANCISCO CA 94133
3C LTRS CR RTS
SYRACUSE NY

.324 three-Digit Carrier Routes Sacks. When, after preparing all Carrier Route and required 5-digit Carrier Routes sacks, there are 125 pieces or 15 pounds or more of qualifying mail to different carrier routes within the same 3-digit ZIP Code area, they MUST be placed in 3-digit Carrier Routes sacks and labeled to the 3-digit ZIP Code destination.

Note: All packages of residual pieces must be placed n 3-digit Carrier Routes sacks labeled to the 3-digit ZIP Code destination. Each 3-digit Carrier Routes sack must be labeled in the following manner:

Line 1: City, State and 3-digit ZIP Code Prefix.
Line 2: Contents followed by the words MIXED CARRIER ROUTES.
Line 3: Office of Mailing.
Sample: BINGHAMTON NY 137
3C FLATS MXD CR RTS
WASHINGTON DC

Note: The following abbreviations may be used on the contents line of sack and pallet labels for carrier route presort rate level mailings:

LETTERS . . . . .LTRS
FLATS. . . . . .FLTS
MIXED . . . . .MXD
DIGIT . . . . .DG
CARRIER ROUTE . . . . .CR
CARRIER ROUTES . . . . .CR RTS
RURAL ROUTE . . . . .RR
POST OFFICE BOX SCTION . . . . .PO BOX SECT
HIGHWAY CONTRACT ROUTE . . . . .HC
GENERAL DELIVERY UNIT . . . . .GD

667.4 Preparation Requirements for 5-Digit Presort Level Rate.

.42 General.

a. Sack Preparation. All packages of 10 or more pieces to the same 5-digit ZIP Code destination must be placed in sacks containing a minimum of 125 pieces or 15 pounds of mail and must be prepared in accordance with 667.421 through 667.423. Mailers must note on the mailing statement submitted with the mailing whether the 125 piece or 15 pounds minimum, or both, were used as the basis for preparing the entire mailing in sacks.

Exceptions:

(1) If authorized to bundle or palletize, mailers must prepare packages and bundles in accordance with 667.5 or 667.6.

(2) Mailers who Express Mail drop ship bulk third-class mailings in accordance with 136.7 may prepare sacks containing fewer than 125 pieces or less than 15 pounds of mail. However, all other preparation requirements must be met to qualify for the 5-digit presort level.

b. Sack Label Color. Sack labels must be white or manila (other colors will not be accepted).

c. Sack Weight. No more than 70 pounds of mail may be placed in any sack.

.421 5-Digit Sacks. When there are 125 pieces or 15 pounds of qualifying 5-digit mail for the same 5-digit destination, it MUST be placed in a 5-digit sack. Five-digit sacks containing fewer than 125 pieces or less than 15 pounds of qualifying mail will NOT be accepted. Each sack must be labeled in the following manner:

Line 1: City, State and 5-digit ZIP Code destination.
Line 2: Contents.
Line 3: Office of Mailing.
Sample: ARLINGTON VA 22202
        3C LTRS
        BOSTON MA

.422 Unique 3-Digit City Sacks. Mailers may commingle different 5-digit packages of 10 or more pieces for unique 3-digit cities listed in Exhibit 122.63b into unique 3-digit city sacks providing:

(a) Each sack contains at least 125 pieces or 15 pounds of mail, and

(b) Three-digit city packages are NOT included in the sack, and

(c) 125 pieces or 15 pounds of mail for a single 5-digit ZIP Code (within the unique 3-digit city) must be sacked separately.

Each unique 3-digit city sack must be labeled in the following manner:

Line 1: City, State and unique 3-digit ZIP Code Prefix.
Line 2: Contents followed by the words "MIXED 5-DIGIT PKGS".
Line 3: Office of Mailing.
Sample: BINGHAMTON NY 139
        3C LTRS MXD 5-DG PKGS
        PHILADELPHIA PA

.423 3-Digit Sacks. When, after preparing all required 5-digit and unique 3-digit city sacks, there are 125 pieces or 15 pounds of qualifying 5-digit mail to different 5-digit ZIP Code destinations within a 3-digit ZIP Code area, it MUST be placed in 3-digit sacks. To qualify for the 5-digit presort level rate there must be a minimum of 50 pieces or 10 pounds of 5-digit mail for any 5-digit ZIP Code separation within the 3-digit sack. ONLY qualifying 5-digit packages may be placed in these 3-digit sacks. Each 3-digit sack must be labeled in the following manner:

Line 1: City, State and 3-digit ZIP Code Prefix.
Line 2: Contents followed by the words "MIXED 5-DIGIT PKGS".
Line 3: Office of Mailing.
Sample: BINGHAMTON NY 137
        3C LTRS MXD 5-DG PKGS
        PHILADELPHIA PA

Note: The following abbreviations may be used on the contents line of sack and pallet labels for 5-digit presort level mailings:

```
LETTERS...............................................LTRS
FLATS.................................................FLTS
MIXED ................................................MXD
DIGIT ................................................DG
```

These changes will be incorporated into a future revision of the DMM.

—Rates & Classification Dept., 4-17-86.

Chapter 3

THE OFFER
Your Advertising Package

YOU HAVE ARRIVED! You have done your homework. You have thought and thought and thought until you are about worn out. I know you were beginning to wonder if you would ever reach this point. Well, the fun now begins. You know it's no fun if you never get to do the project. So let's do it. You can begin to think and dream about how to advertise your product. How are you going to advertise your product? We will begin by first learning about an advertising package or matrix.

The creative package consists of five or six pieces: the outer envelope, the brochure, the sales letter, the order card and sometimes a warranty or guarantee card, and the return envelope or BRE. I told you earlier that there are some places you can skimp a bit but this isn't the place. Here it's your best foot forward. That sounds simple enough—the trick is getting the best you can afford for professional help to put the package together for you. There are fine advertising agencies that can help you here, with a wide range from very reasonable prices to very expensive. Again I caution you to go slow. Talk to several agencies, find out their price and their time schedule, and find one you will have good rapport with. (Over the years I have been privileged to have the best.)

First of all, if you can't afford an agency at least find a good writer, a local artist and a production specialist such as the team of Herschell and Margo Lewis. Frankly, that makes you the actual manager of the project. By overseeing everything yourself, you can save lots of money. Below is a chart that will help you produce your schedule. Seeing your product unfold is thrilling. At last you really start to believe you are going to do it. Instead of Las Vegas being the house, you are!

DESIGN/PRODUCTION

Name   Job Number
Department   Date
Project   Date Required
Request for: rough layout
             finished layout
             production art
             number to be printed

Circle number of colors   one   two   three   four   five   six   other

NAME OF PROJECT
PROJECT REPORT SHEET

MARKETING COMPONENTS

COMPONENTS SEQUENCE	DATE DUE	DATE COMPLETED
COPY:		
Letter	_____	_____
Brochure	_____	_____
Special Insert	_____	_____
Order Card	_____	_____
Other Envelope	_____	_____
Reply Envelope	_____	_____
Layout:		
Rough Layout	_____	_____
Final Layout	_____	_____
Production-Series:		
Art Decision	_____	_____
Transparencies	_____	_____
Color Separations	_____	_____
Blue Line Proof	_____	_____
Print	_____	_____
Insertions	_____	_____
Drop	_____	_____
Mailing List:		
List Selection	_____	_____
List Reservation	_____	_____
Tape labels to merge purge	_____	_____
Send house list to be supressed	_____	_____

Labels to Printer-affix   _____   _____
Order acknowledgement:
     Letter   _____   _____
     Outer Envelope   _____   _____
Mailing procedure:
     Insert components per matrix   _____   _____
     Deliver to post office drop   _____   _____

Product Production:
     Container for product   _____   _____
     Select Art (for boxes)   _____   _____
     Take to artist   _____   _____
     Art proof approved   _____   _____
     Boxes ordered   _____   _____
     Box received   _____   _____
     Selection of product   _____   _____
     Take to artist   _____   _____
     Art proof approved   _____   _____
     Product into plant or Warehouse   _____   _____
     Product Shipped   _____   _____

Product Fulfillment:
     On top of the box:
         Outer envelope with window   _____   _____
         Invoice   _____   _____
         Return envelope   _____   _____
         Others (certificates, pink sheets-
            story sheets-back sell of
            product)   _____   _____

Insert programs:
     Art   _____   _____
     Copy   _____   _____
     Insert production/printing   _____   _____
     Order form   _____   _____
     Return envelope   _____   _____

Space program:
     Determine media schedule   _____   _____
     Determine camera ready due date   _____   _____
     Reserve space   _____   _____
     Production AD:
         copy   _____   _____
         art   _____   _____
     To engraver   _____   _____
     Mechanical to publisher   _____   _____

     Track back end and fulfill   _____   _____

Now, let's talk about what should be on each piece of the mailing matrix and how it should appear when your prospective customer opens the mailing piece.

THE OUTER ENVELOPE. This is the first approach you have to your customer. This will be their first impression. Does it look good enough to open, or will they toss it in file 13? Make it so appealing that they can't wait to open it.

Let's take the front of the envelope first. You will notice at the top right of the envelope the word "indicia". This is one of the post office requirements for bulk rate mailings. The number will indicate the city where the mail has been mailed. Try to arrange for a universal permit number so that you can mail anywhere within the United States with just this one number, not several different numbers. Then you will have the three traditional lines:

Mr. and Mrs. F. Smith
2407 Meadow Lark Lane
Springfield, Texas 78500   12345-3122

Out to the right of the zip is another set of numbers we will call the key identification. This number can be from 3 to 5 digits.

The Offer

In Chapter Four we will go into greater detail about the key number. For now we will simply say that each list that you have will be identified by a set of numbers so that you will know where the sale originated. The key number will go on the outer envelope and also on the order card. On the outer envelope you will also have your return address. Once you have your house list, use below the indicia the words "Correct Address Return Requested." When you are renting a list, it is not cost effective to have advertising material returned. However, when you have your house list it will be important to keep the addresses of your customer current. This service costs about 25¢ for each corrected customer address. The above cover the basics to be put on the outer envelope. Now, you can put anything else that your heart desires or that will draw the person into the mailing piece such as "Open me here", or "a free gift for you is inside." Also art work can be applied as well to indicate to your reader what great deal they will have if they will just look inside. Or leave it plain and official looking.

The most popular size of the mailing brochure is one of the standard paper sizes, one example being 6 × 9 when folded and placed into the envelope. These papers are easier to get and cost much less. But you may not want to do that. So design what you want. Just be sure that there is a paper supplier that can produce them and a letter shop that has the correct machinery so that the piece can be processed.

In Chapter Five, we will discuss the printer and production in great detail.

Now, let's move to the back of the envelope. Again, here is a place to have art work of your product. After deciding on envelope sizes you will have the type size to consider and the color of the paper and ink. It has been proven that white paper with black ink and number 8 size type is a good selection. Try to stay away from anything smaller than a type size 6. The larger the type, the better. Unfortunately, with large type you can't say as much. On the other hand, your prospective customer will be able to read it. Colored paper is a good idea for your mailing piece, though you will have to pay more for it. As for colors, remember that warm tones make people react. Pinks, yellows, bright greens, and reds are wonderful. Cool colors such as light blue and light green turn people off. Black paper with white ink is popular although white paper with black ink still holds the number one winner's spot for response. You don't see the black paper with white ink often: nevertheless, it is true! Oftentimes you will want to use several colors of ink.

THE BROCHURE. Here is a great place to show your product. Be sure the colors are right, in proper focus, and the printing in line. I have seen so many brochures where you couldn't even see the picture because it was so fuzzy. Illustrated below are some of the brochures I have used through the years that have been eagles (winners). Turkeys Don't Fly—But Eagles Soar. It is true that a picture is worth a thousand words. Be an Eagle....

Here are some of the features you should have on the brochure:

Clear shot of the product (Make sure it is in register)
Benefits the customer will receive
Return address
Telephone number
Uniqueness of product
Guarantee
Easy methods of payment

THE LETTER. Lots of thought here. Some people feel a two-page letter front and back is long enough. If you have an elaborate brochure, I'm inclined to agree. On the other hand, if your brochure is simple, a four-page letter is a must. You may think that is too long, but I promise you that's how long it takes to secure your customer. The more your prospective customer reads and knows about the product, the more excited he/she will become. The letter should be direct and to the point. It should contain your warranty statement if you are not going to have a warranty card. Then fill it up with as much back-up material as you can get on the page. A good form for the letter is: (illustration)

Be sure the letter contains the benefits, the price, the product's importance, how to buy it, the warranty statement and your telephone number.

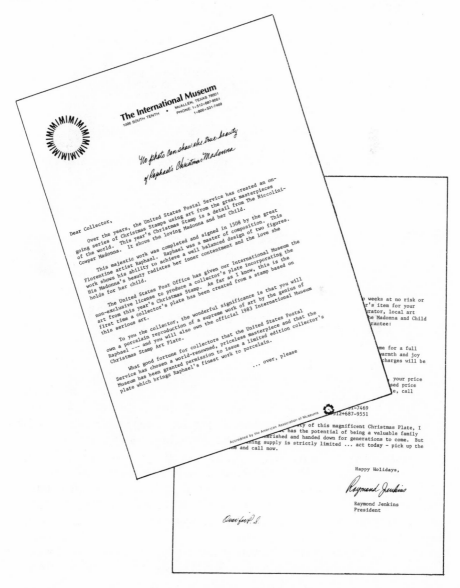

THE ORDER CARD. The bottom line. . . . This is it. This is where you get the customer. Make it easy and clear to read, with a place to sign, and an enumeration of benefits again. Be sure the key code is on it for identification, your phone number (800 number preferably), and credit card information with the customer's signature line. A signature line in red is good. That's where you want your customer to sign his/her name—anything to get the customer to react. Give plenty of space for the customer to fill in for additional orders.

WARRANTY CARD. Now this really isn't necessary but a nice touch if you can swing it. The guarantee or warranty card states plainly that if your customer doesn't want to keep the product he/she can send it back. There should be a stated length of time the customer has to decide about keeping the product, and a full refund should be offered. A warranty card does give prestige to a mailing. If you don't have a warranty card enclosed, be sure the warranty statement is somewhere in the letter and on the brochure. This gives credibility to your business. Some companies give 15 days, 30 days or even one year.

On this subject, I had a funny thing happen. When I moved into a larger office, we were re-doing our list and in the shipping record there appeared to be a lady who had never bothered to pay her bill. What perplexed us was how this had been allowed to happen. Bingo, there it was: she kept trading for a new plate each year, with her warranty agreement. She would decide after a year (she had enjoyed it, you know) she'd return it for credit. Then she'd send for another one. This must have gone on for three years. There was nothing illegal—she had simply taken advantage of a loophole. Well, that did it. We changed the policy a bit to include that if this happened more than twice, perhaps it might be considered a possible sale, and the customer must pay for at least one plate. It seems that no matter what you do, someone can get around it.

RETURN ENVELOPE, OR BRE: As you can see on the illustration on page 48, in the upper right-hand corner is the permit number. Now you only use this if you are going to pay for the returned order form. It does give you a slight edge to pay for the return order. Nothing says that you have to but over time prepaid postage on orders shows a slight edge in response. I have done it both ways. If you do decide to use this system, the procedure is to set up something like a bank account at the post office. They have you put money in the account much in the same way as you do in a bank. Then as the orders come into the post office, the postman deducts the amount from the existing account. When you run out, you put in more money and so on. It is a nice way to do business. And of course be sure the company name and address is on the return BRE. Depending on how many tests you are running, the return envelopes or the ink on them can be of different colors. You need something to identify the mailing in an instant. Simple, and it saves much confusion.

How does the matrix fit into the envelope? Mail is ordinarily opened from the back. Packing the envelope should anticipate this. If you want the mail opened differently one method is putting a flap over the front; thus the customer will open it from the front. First should be the letter, then the brochure, the order card, the warranty card, and—tucked away nicely—the BRE.

THE BUSINESS REPLY ENVELOPE (BRE)

The steps involved in creating your mailing piece will be discussed in greater detail in Chapter Five. For now, let us quickly go over them. If you hire an advertising agency or if you do the project yourself the procedure will be the same. If you decide to use an agency for your project it will get turned over to an account executive. First will be your idea. Then you will relate that to an artist (the concept). Second will be what I call a cartoon. This is a drawing in super rough form that puts the matrix together. Again, if you use an agency or not, you should check each thing as it is completed. Thirdly, you will see the actual art and the specific place it is to be placed.

Fourth will be the lithographs of the product. A lithograph is a transparency of the product that has been photographed four times, one time with each of the primary colors—yellow, blue, red—plus the color black. Combinations of these have all the colors that will be necessary for your mailing.

Fifth will be the chromolins or striping production. These are what the printer will actually print from. They have everything in place—the copy, artwork, and colors. Then you will have a print run. Not every piece that you will produce will be a four-color job. Sometimes you may just want a one- or two-color project. It is cheaper, and for some products maybe black and white is more appropriate. Check your prices and see.

Instead of a brochure for what we call a single sale item, you might decide to do a catalogue. The components can be the same or slightly different in approach from the "multiple mailing piece" matrix. If you send a catalogue without a cover envelope, it must still have tucked inside it the BRE, the order card, the warranty statement, sales copy to sell the items, and the 800 number. You have seen them—Saks, Neiman Marcus, Horchow, etc.

The Offer

Some catalogues use an outer envelope, with all the same positioning as the solo mailing. Other types of mailings are the self mailer, the telegram, the mailogram, etc. Only one type of mailing I know of doesn't use a BRE—the negative option. You will come across the explanation for the negative option in Chapter Twelve.

After you have decided what style you are going to use, make a decision on the longevity of this mailing—a continuity program mailing, a one shot, an open end, or a limited edition. With a continuity program, as we discussed in Chapter Two, your mail order business can shine. The expense in mail order is obtaining the first order. Anything you can do to sell your customer more than one item on a regular basis is the big secret. Continuity!!!!!

A one shot is exactly what it sounds like. You make the sale one time, win or lose. Not too many people I know can make it like this. You will see space ads that fit this category: "Buy the waist thinner today". You have one item to sell—that's it. Your expenses are riding on one shot as well. Once you have a customer and you have a second product that might interest your customer, then you can have a continuity program. Collectors fit well into this category. Also food fanciers. (I can't live without steak from Omaha Steaks. I'm hooked). People who like to eat will buy their products over and over again. People will buy things in a series such as Book-of-the-Month Club provides or commemorative editions companies can offer. Any time you can sell more than one item to a customer you have a long-lasting business.

Below is a one shot ad with a continuity program to back it up.

Chapter 4

THE ALL-IMPORTANT LIST
It's Who You Know

The list is how you will build your business. In the beginning Sears struck on the idea that they would go to the customer by putting a catalogue together and sending it through the mail to "Dear Occupant". When Dear Occupant wrote in an order, Sears kept it, and it became their "House List". Years later, a friend of mine came up with the idea to convince major businesses in and about the old USA to let him put their house lists into a rental pool. The companies had to be willing to rent their house lists to other companies that wouldn't be competing with their existing products. *Voila!* It came to pass and a new successful business was born. Businesses could make a nice profit renting their house lists to other companies so they could grow as well. Thus list rental began.

There are several very fine list houses, with fine list brokers, in and around Chicago and New York and the west coast. These houses rent on a large scale but are willing to start small and grow with you as your company grows. Brokers know that if they pick the right list for you, they will make money too. There are other smaller companies that rent specialty lists, lists of universities, or ham radio operators, or veterans. It just depends on what type of direct marketing you plan to be in. The list broker makes approximately 15% of the cost of the list. So if a list rents for $65 a thousand, the broker will make 15% of the $65. Lists are rented in lots of a thousand. The industry refers to them as per thousand. You might think that renting your list to other companies would be detrimental and indeed some firms feel that way and won't rent their list; however, the direct marketing world has proven that time after time people who buy by mail buy many items by mail and still buy from the original company. In fact, this practice makes a stronger mail-order person. So these repeat multi-buyers are the backbone of the mail order trade. Besides names that are rented, other names are traded. Sometimes this is done between private companies, one on one and nothing more. Besides brokered and traded house lists, there is a group of names we call "compiled." These names are not known mail order buyers of a particular product but they have bought something in the market place such as a car or license plate, or have been to a trade show or a convention. Of course, the response on such a list will be much smaller than that for house lists.

List brokers are worth their weight in gold. Their role is to put together what lists they feel will be most beneficial in the sale of your product. It is very important to start with their help from the beginning for many valid reasons. One, you just can't mail a million pieces of advertising at first. Here is where mail order science comes into play. The first thing you will do along with the guidance of the list broker is decide how many customers you want the first mailing. Then, you will put together a group comprised of from 5000 to 6000 names from each list or business that you want to rent from. At this point, it may be difficult to control your enthusiasm and greed. You must realize that building your business takes careful thought. You must start with a controlled test. If you want to start out with the optimum test I say no more than 100,000-125,000 names. That usually is comprised of 20 to 30 lists. No one says you have to do so many and in fact, you may begin with as few as five lists. (Refer to Chapter Two for response levels.) Remember that a one percent response would be 1000 orders if you mail 100,000 names. That's a good way to start. If you are only wanting 100 customers, then mail 10,000 names. But actually a one percent response is an optimum response. Depending on what you are selling, the range can be anywhere from .002 (twenty order response) per thousand upwards. So figure for the worst and the best you think you can achieve. Don't be discouraged by these figures—if you have done your homework well you probably will fall anywhere from .005 to a .01. Sometimes more expensive products bring a lower response. These are strong and good responses. Think how many customers it will take to cover your costs, with a living thrown in. It depends on what you are willing to settle for. Remember you are in the business to make money so be sure you are asking enough for your product. A good rule of thumb is to charge three to four times the cost you have in your product. Hard as it may seem to understand, if the cost is too low, people won't think it's good quality.

Another important point here is that maybe you will only want 100 customers, but you may be able to sell them several items or the same item several times during the year. Your customer's sales have now fallen into the bracket of automatic shipments. A good example of this is the limited edition field. The Franklin Mint and Book-of-the-Month Club are highly successful examples of sequential mail order selling.

If you look back in Chapter Two at the successful mailing matrix, you see now why it is so important to fill in the chart. The list broker will mail to you several sheets with information about each business he/she thinks will work for you. Here's a list broker's sample information sheet. These information sheets will be your guide to your first cold mailing and for your continuation mailings thereafter.

TRIBUTE (Name of Company)   99577

24,999	SUBSCRIBERS	$85.00/M	DATE 04/88
INQUIRE	MONTHLY HOTLINE	$95.00/M	SEX 64% MALE
55,000	LONG TERM SUBSCRIBERS	$85.00/M	ADDRESSING
2,000	MONTHLY CHANGE OF ADDRESS	$80.00/M	CHESHIRE-4UP
			M/T 800/1600
			P.S. LABELS
			$6.00/M
			KEY CODING
			$1.50/M

PROFILE: MONTHLY CONSULTING MAGAZINE. FEATURES HELPFUL DETAIL TO BE SUCCESSFUL IN THE DIRECT MARKETING FIELD.

UNIT	$20.00	SELECTIONS
		NTH NAME N/C
		ST/SCF/ZIP $2.50/M
		SEX $5.00/M
		MINIMUM: 5000
		SAMPLE REQUIRED

SOURCE: DIRECT MAIL (98%)
NOTE: ORDERS CANCELLED AFTER MAIL DATE OR 5 DAYS BEFORE MAIL DATE WILL BE CHARGED FULL PRICE.

As I said earlier, arrange to have key numbers assigned to each list. The key number will be how you track your orders to see which lists did well for you when the orders are finally in your office. The key number will determine how you will mail in the future. Once these key numbers are applied to the individual list, the next thing is to order the names by "nth."

This means that you want to rent every tenth name on that list, the idea being a good cross section of possible customers. The next thing you want to do is give the list broker several names of friends and acquaintances to place on different lists so that you know those names really got mailed. This is called seeding the list. Unfortunately, some pieces of mail don't drop (get mailed). The post office does an outstanding job but occasionally a shipment of mail is lost. In a recent study (1987), the test drop proved unfortunately that no improvements have been made since 1983. That is an alarming fact. The new Postmaster General says he is working on it. Something is awry.

The way to know that each list was mailed is to key each list. You will have a list in your office to check against plus you may want a firm such as The Monitor to track these mailings for you as you grow. It's a good service and it's very important. What recourse do you have if no orders come off a list? You might suspect it didn't get mailed. Call your letter shop—have them go over to the post office and look for the sacks of mail for you. The letter shop, which we will discuss in the next chapter, does all these little clean-up items. I have really been lucky through the years. Only once did I know that my mailing didn't get in the post office when it was scheduled. In fact, I went to court over it and won. In this case, the letter shop was at fault for not honoring our agreed-upon mail date. If it ever happens to you sue for telephone numbers (at least one million dollars) as my attorney did. You may not get a million dollars but you should get paid for your damages and you will get the letter shop's attention. It's not nice to play around with a mail date: missing a mail date is serious business. Many letter shop companies say: "That's just too bad". This company was careless and disregarded the fact that it takes months to set up a list rental and that once I missed that date I might not be able to rent the list again for several more months . . . the reason being that the list has been rented to some other company. There I was with all that paper and no place for it to be mailed. Mad doesn't begin to explain my emotions. So learn from my experience. Stand over them with glue.

The mail date is so important and the rental process so revered that a mix up is considered a major blooper. Once just such a thing occurred when a company misunderstood about their mail date. Our names were being rented along with several other companies'. The mistake was uncovered after the mailing was sent. The company personally called each list owner and explained what had happened and asked for forgiveness. As far as I know, no owner sued but the company who rented the different company lists promised they would be more careful in the future. Each company wants protection of at least 3 weeks' grace period on each side of the mail date so they can use exclusively their own list and ones they have rented and have a good shot at selling their new offer.

Mail Order on the Kitchen Table

The companies that you have rented a list from will send their names to your list broker. He will have them put through a system called merge purge. My friend Alan Drey worked many hard hours getting this system established. What it does is run all the lists against themselves and kick out the names that are duplicated. You can see immediately how valuable a tool this is. It saves having to have many more than enough mailing pieces printed and paying postage on duplicates. The money savings can be astronomical. The other thing it does is begin a history of your business, so that when you want to have a continuation mailing you can go back and see what you did before. The merge purge will give you information such as how many names were originally submitted, the actual amount mailed from that list, the multi-buyers, the number of names sent to each state, how many women and how many men, which names were used from a particular list such as "nth" names, and so on. Here is where I should mention submerged house lists. Once you begin having customers, you surely don't want to rent these names again. So you run your house list, key code it—say 1000—and send it through the merge purge. You ask the merge purge to suppress your list, that is, disallow or kick out all names on the list you are renting that you already have for current customers. Let's say you are going to rent two lists plus add your house list.

They would be coded this way:

House List (your existing customers)	1000
Tribute	0001
Gallery	0002

and so on. That way you don't go to the expense of getting the names you already own.

There are several ways these lists can come from the list broker. The letter shop will put the names in two places in the mailing, one on the outer envelope or letter and one on the order form. The names of a company can come on (1) cheshire labels—names sent on a sheet of paper which the letter shop will cut and paste on the mailing piece; (2) magnetic tape—a computer tape process that allows the letter shop to take the name directly typed to the mailing piece; or (3) pressure-sensitive labels—labels applied directly to the mailing piece. These labels have sticky backing and can be applied to mailing pieces by hand in your office. Many companies are now using two other methods, the catalogue method where the customer must pull the label off the front of the catalog and place it on the order card and the laser method, where the ink shoots the name directly on the mailing piece.

List protection is of course the biggest concern of the company renting the list. Therefore, just for your information, if you were to use the list a second time without their permission, you will be sued for millions. Theft! Scary! You really have to play it right and that's the job of your list broker as well. Sometimes a company will not keep its list updated. This can be a nightmare. A name, an address, or state can be incorrect and you have spent a fortune on your print production! The mailing piece that doesn't reach its destination because of wrong information in the address is known as a nixie. Nixies are costly and worrisome. So be careful who you rent from, and who you have rent for you. The list broker's job is to keep abreast of any inkling about a company that might not be keeping its house list up to date.

Now, how long will all this take? Will you believe me when I tell you at least four to six months? Once you determine what you want to sell and then call the list broker, his job will begin by his getting in contact with the list company whose list you want to rent. Then the first thing that company will do is check you out. They will want to see a sample of your mailing piece. This is to be sure it is first class. After they accept that, they will want to check your credit. Sometimes when you are a new client, they will ask for cash up front. Finally, they will check to see if they are going to use the list themselves then, or perhaps they have already agreed to let another company rent it at that time. Then they will have to notify your broker with the information. If you clear all of the roadblocks they will set up a run date. So plan well ahead in order to save you time and money. It is important to get all the lists to the list broker at the same time for a successful merge purge. The list broker usually handles this transaction from the list owners but once in a while you might have to help out. It seems in almost every mailing at least one list is late. So give yourself plenty of time. When the lists have been run through the merge purge, the list broker will send them to the letter shop. The broker will give you information from the merge purge such as input (all the names you have rented), output (what was left after duplicate names, bad addresses, etc), the multibuyers (buyers who buy from more than one list), how many names you have rented by states, and any other requests for information you have given him, such as demographies (where the names come from), a breakdown by sex, and so on. Then he will send you the bill.

Well, have fun with your list, but be careful. This is where your judgement can make or break you. Use the list broker—he may be the most valuable tool you will have.

Chapter 5

PRINTING AND MAILING
Getting Help

Now that you have arranged for your mailing list, you will be embarking on a printing adventure. A printing shop can perform a multitude of functions for you. There are three main types of print shops/mailing houses—those who deal in single sheet printing called letter press, those who deal in continuous forms called offset printing (using the web press), and those who do gravure printing. Before you decide what type will fit your needs, you will have to know how many pieces you want to have printed. Most smaller mailings will be done by a print shop with letter press single-sheet printing machines, but there is a point where that's no longer economical. When this situation occurs, then it is best to use the continuous form procedure—offset. The gravure is not one you will likely be using as a beginner because this procedure is used only for extremely large printings. Whichever way you decide to go, you will use the following steps:

Step 1. COMPOSITION: Birthing a job. This is the idea you come up with. This is the design stage. Here you should have what I call a cartoon of your idea in mock-up form. The cartoon includes the copy and art work of the sales letter, the outer envelope, the return envelope, the brochure and the warranty card. This will give you an idea of how everything will fit into the mailing matrix. Then you will take actual pictures of your product, the illustrations. The next procedure is either a chromolin (all 4 colors of the separations meshed together to appear as one piece) or each of the four colors on separate sheets laid over each other (called stripping) to get the correct color of what you want to see in the finished picture. The purpose for these two types of proofing is so the printer will have the correct color, the position to fit on the press, and the quality of the piece.

You will want to check each of the above stages yourself as every person has his own idea of the way things should be. It is your mailing; have

56

the colors as you think they should be. Check your proof. In fact, check everything with a fine eye. Once you sign the printer's proof, you will have had your last chance to change anything. If the color isn't color perfect, have them do it over. Once you are satisfied then the next step is called camera-ready—meaning the art work is ready for making the negatives that will print your mailing piece. So far this procedure is the same for the single sheet letter press printing, offset continuous forms, or the gravure method. The print shop takes the chromolin or the four single sheet overlay and puts it into a large camera. Here they shoot the negative. In other words, a picture of the art work is taken and a negative made from it. Here also is where the art work is enlarged or made smaller. The negative is then developed. This is where the procedure takes a different turn. You may decide whether to print by means of letter press, offset, or gravure.

In the beginning it is best for you to start with letter press. From here on, we may occasionally refer to offset because eventually you will be using that method. But, most of the time we will be referring to letter press.

Step 2. ARRANGING THE PRINTING. Once your layout or paste-up is camera-ready, you order your paper and color of ink from the printer. At this point you will need to decide which way you want to print. First, let me explain that letter press single-sheet printing can print as high as 300,000 pieces. The point then that will help you decide what method to go will be price of paper, the time involved, and the convenience of the print shop. The differences in letter press and offset lithography are clear. Letter press printing takes much longer,and therefore can be much more costly than offset. Continuous form (the paper comes in one continuous roll and is printed that way—not, individual sheets) can be printed at much higher rates of speed, so on large runs probably offset continuous form will be more beneficial. Letter press makes sharp, very clear type images. The letter press can use twice the ink film thickness of lithography and can be used to print metallic inks and fluorescent materials. The offset can use inexpensive intermediate plates whereas in the letterpress method, those are much more costly and may use more labor.

The next thing that will help you decide which printing method to use is the weight of the paper. Letter press can print almost anything in paper weight where the offset continuous form (the Web press) prints from 57-pound up to 60-pound paper. Also the continuous form runs up to 24 points board thick. Paper is measured in both bond and board. 60-pound bond and 60-pound board are different in thickness. The pound paper as you go higher in the number has more body, more fiber per inch. Board is measured in the same way.

There are two methods to weigh paper: point and pound. They are different in that point is measured by thousandths of an inch thick, not weight, and pound is measured by the weight of the paper. You can buy paper in any weight or points and grade. Be sure here about the price break. A price break is where the weight of the paper changes the price per thousand purchased. Sometimes 60-pound paper can serve the same purpose as 70-pound paper, and it is cheaper. When you're making a large mailing, it can be this small difference in paper weight that can save you money and make the difference in your gross cost.

The printer will need lead time so be sure that you "pencil in" at least six months ahead of your mailing date for large orders. "Penciling in" is a term meaning you think that's when you're going to want to mail. After you definitely decide on a date you will ask the printer to "ink you in." That means your printing date is a concrete time. In making your decision on which print method to use, you need to have a contract with them to have printed just what you want printed. When you say you want 10,000 envelopes, you want to get 10,000 envelopes. If you read the fine print in your contract with the printer, you will notice that he can make mistakes. That is, he may deliver you less than the quantity you specify, by a certain percentage, or he may print more, by a certain percentage, than you ordered, in which case you may be obliged to pay for the total printing. Read your printer's contract carefully. This is all important. You must insist on having a contract that states that the printer won't underrun the amount you want manufactured, and that he won't overrun more than 5% of production. The importance here is that if you rent 10,000 names you want to mail 10,000 names and not 9,000 names. You have planned your mailing response on the 10,000 number and your response could be substantially off if the printing job is in error. Also if you have in the contract the 5% agreement, then you don't have to pay the printing difference for high overruns. Can you imagine what that can do for your pocket book? When you plan how many matrixes (complete mailing pieces) you will need to mail, be sure you include some number that you will want for your office. It is fun to have a few samples lying around for your friends and family to see.

Step 3. BURNING THE PLATES. At this point, the images on the film are burned into a set of plates which will be attached to the printing press. Burning the plates represents an irrevocable step in the process. You would not want to find a glaring error after the plates are burned, for it would be very expensive to do this step again.

Step 4. PRINTING. I'm sure there are many more types of letter press machines out in the field, but we are only going to talk about four: A B

Dick, Chief, Merge, and Heidelberg. The first two, A B Dick and the Chief, use one color at a time. Papers are re-fed into the machine as many times as there are colors on your matrix. Letter press machines are really duplicators, working on the same principle as the old mimeograph machine in your high school principal's office.

The "Heid" runs a single color at a time, so for a four-color piece it must run the piece four times, one for each of the four colors. As the paper is printing, there is a constant check for correct color density.

The "Merge" can do two colors at a time—yellow and black first, then red and blue. The machine has a feeder, then two ink presses and a drying bin and collector. A fine powder is dusted on the pieces before they are stacked and collated. This helps the printed piece to dry and not stick to the next piece that comes off the press.

In this field of duplicators is also the New Xerox 990. But with it you have to print larger numbers and you can only get one color. Commercially the "Merge" and the "Heid" are used. They print all sorts of brochures, folders, and advertising material.

Step 5. BINDING. This is the final product from the presses. Involved are folding, cutting, and bursting. Bursting is simply another word for separating the continuous forms of the mailing. The offset web press system has automatic knives to cut the printed piece into separate parts. (The letter press system requires another machine). The web offset machine is set for automatic cutting and bursting while the other type machines must have someone to manually hold the paper and turn it. This gets the same job done but at a much slower rate. Folding on the web press doesn't need to be on another machine either. It has knives that are used for folding. There may be as many as 4 knives that are used. Letter press doesn't have this feature. After the printed piece goes through the first cut and the folding process, the printer will put the piece back on the cutter and trim off all the bad spots so you will have a smooth job.

Be sure you begin a scrapbook at this point. You will want all of the printing matrixes along with the price for each piece underneath. You will want to keep a record of the weight of the paper, the printer whom you used and the date. Also keep notes on whether the print shop was timely, pleasant, efficient, and fulfilled the terms of the contract.

Whichever method you use for printing, be sure everything you will need for your mailing matrix is at the printer at the same time. This is important for two reasons: 1) so pieces can all be run at the same time (called gang run), and 2) to keep down additional start-up costs. If you are on time with all the parts of your matrix, you not only save the printer's time, but you have a chance of a smooth job. Again, Murphy can get in the way here. I have had experiences where I rented a list and was all set for a certain number of envelopes and order form cards to be run. But at the last minute, more names came in than I had expected because the merge purge didn't kick out as many dupes as I had thought it would. I ended up needing 3500 more mailing pieces. I might mention here that when you are running a merge purge you can usually expect about 8% to 10% of the names to be dupes or bad addresses. Sometimes when you are running a first direct marketing test this number can be substantially lower, due to the fact you have rented nth names and only five thousand, not twenty-five thousand. With the lower number, you don't have as many duplicate names—it just seems to work that way. The more names that you rent, the higher the chance to run into dupes or bad addresses. There's a very complicated law of averages here that need not concern us too much, except to notice how the percent of bad names will vary with the over-all number of names ordered.

If you find yourself short, you pray for the 5% overrun, or you frantically call the printer and see what he's got in his little bag of tricks. If you are lucky, he's bought more paper than he thought he'd need—thinking he might mess up—and you are saved. If not, hopefully you planned way ahead and can get more paper so as not to mess up your mail date. It has been known to happen . . . No one said you wouldn't have a few breathless moments. As a professor said to me once before an organ performance when I said I was a tad nervous, "That way you know you are alive." If after your first list test, you plan to do a continuation mailing, (or "roll out", as it is called) you may opt to purchase what paper you think you will need for both jobs. The benefit here is that the paper for both runs will be cheaper if bought at one time. The disadvantage is that you will probably have to pay for the paper in advance.

You will just have to see what looks best for your pocketbook. I have done it both ways. Frankly, I like to buy what I need at the time. If your mailing bombs, you surely don't want to own all that paper. Even if your mailing is wildly successful, you can eke along better doing the purchasing in small bites, especially if you don't plan to do the continuation mailing for several months. Your money can be tied up in paper when you could have the money at the bank making a few more dollars for you so that you could mail a larger list. Some paper manufacturers will grant you credit if they know you will continue mailing with them over the long haul. And if you find you're in a financial bind, they will be willing to work with you. One way is to borrow their money and pay them interest. I've done that too.

Make sure the print shop and the letter shop are running on schedule, along with the receiving of the magnetic tapes or pressure sensitive labels from your list broker. Remember we discussed in Chapter Four that lists will arrive at the letter shop by three methods. However, if you want all the lists to go through merge purge at the same time, the names will have to be placed onto a magnetic tape. But there is always a list or two you want that can't be set up on magnetic tape. These will be sent to the letter shop on either pressure-sensitive labels or cheshire labels. The coordination of the arrival of all the lists at the print shop and the delivery by the printer of the mailing pieces is known as dovetailing. It takes a special talent, patience and sometimes knocking a few heads to get it pulled off. But, whatever it takes, do it. After all, it is your money, your mailing, and your mail date.

Step 6. MAILING. After the printing, you are into the last segment before you actually drop your mailing. ("Drop" means the actual mailing piece going into the mail). The letter shop cleans up all the last minute things, such as a magnetic mailing list tape being late. Aside from addressing your mailing piece, the letter shop provides the service of sacking, bagging, sorting, and tying. This job can be monumental if you try to do it, especially for the kind of quantities I hope you eventually will have. But in small quantities you can do it—I have. If you live close to a letter shop but they only address, and your quantity is small, then refer to Chapter Two concerning the post office. You will need to follow those instructions to get your mailing piece to the post office. The larger letter shops will provide that service for you. They will require your postage up front before you mail. They will also take care of getting your mailing permit in the city where the mail will drop.

Once in the early days we met a great lady who agreed to do our letter shop work for us. We wanted to mail from our hometown and that was quite agreeable with her. She even agreed to deliver the mail ready for the post office to our plant. Little did I know how much mail we were talking about! It was mountain high. She drove up in a rather large truck, opened the door, and jumped out with a pipe in her hands. Anyone who went through that experience deserved to be fast friends. Years later she presented us with two lemon-spotted spaniels as a reminder of our first meeting. What a wonderful picture I have of this fine gal. She is a hard worker and you know if she says your mail will drop Sept. 11, it will drop. Thank heavens for good letter shops!

As you see, printing, packaging, and mailing can be done in one or several different cities. Find what works better for you. And do as much or as little as you have time and money for. Look around for the best deal.

Chapter 6

GETTING SET FOR SELLING
Coming Through With the Product

In the beginning, all you could do was think and dream about the product you would sell. You are now turning that dream into a reality. You had to let the product take a bit of a back seat while you threw all your energy and time into planning your advertising campaign piece. Now that you have that tall marketing order behind you, have another look at your product.

No doubt, before you started your advertising marketing, you found a source for the product you are going to sell, determined its availability, and fixed a reasonable but profitable retail price for it.

Besides having found a company who is producing your product, you must now also decide where and how that product is to be shipped to your customers. There are at least three ways that you can fulfill your shipping needs. You can (1) actually do the warehousing and ship the product yourself (2) drop ship all your product that is warehoused on another site by a fulfillment operation, or (3) drop ship several different products from several fulfillment sites.

Fulfillment simply put means a business that provides services to complete your business that you don't want to do or don't have the ways and means to complete. Fulfillment operations can provide several different services. If you want only to do the marketing of your product and nothing more, a fulfillment house will for a price provide the following services: 1) ship your product, 2) collect the money from your customers 3) and do customer correspondence.

One advantage of doing the shipping from your office site is that you have the control. Frankly, I prefer this method because I just like actual hands-on. You have the power to plan your shipping times whereas another supplier or fulfillment house is shipping your product at the time schedule of that business. However, if the product is not grown or manufactured in your area and the cost would be prohibitive to have it shipped to you and then reshipped to your customers, perhaps it's better and cheaper to send your labels to a fulfillment company for product shipment to your customer. Cost effective is the name of the game or just plain conveyance. So the choices are varied but interesting . . . you choose.

I found out that there were other companies out there who didn't want to do their shipping so I did the fulfillment for them. It's a nice way to help pay some of your overhead. Anyway, it puts you in charge. Now that you have determined your shipping method, what quantity of your product should you order from your supplier or manufacturer?

There are several ways to figure this. Remember in Chapter Two where the .002 response is outlined? You might make an educated guess from these clues. Or if the product is easily accessible, order what you will need after your responses come in. If you purchase more than your orders turn out to be, and if the product isn't dated material, these leftovers from your first shipment can be sold in additional continuation or new marketing efforts.

Timing or lead time is the critical factor. In my commemorative plate business, I did continuation series that required complicated art work, manufacturing such as printing of decals and casting of dies with a number of moveable parts. Sometimes I would need 18 months' lead time, and perhaps you will too. The lead time is the actual time it takes to get the product you will need for your direct marketing sales. If it's fruit on the trees, then the product can be harvested just before shipment. Still the groves must be reserved well in advance. Once you have your first cold mailing response in the house, you will be more accurate in your product purchases. The first time truly is the hardest: order as short as you possibly can.

If you have to buy your product well ahead of your shipment date, how do you pay for it? One way, of course, is simple direct payment—if you did your math correctly and set up a bank loan to take care of your initial outlay. Or perhaps you have arranged to make a down payment to your supplier with 30 to 60 days to pay out for the product after delivery. Sixty days is a real help as far as cash flow is concerned. By the end of two months you will have most of your payments from your customers in the house so that you can pay your supplier without having had to borrow as much money from the bank, let alone pay that added interest.

You now have your product well in hand. How do you actually ship it? What kind of container will you be using? The supply ideas are endless. My only advice here is to see what is substantial so your product will arrive safely, and use popular box or shipping container sizes that are not out of sight in cost.

Mail Order on the Kitchen Table

A container with personalization or special art work is going to cost you more money. If you just can't live without it, go ahead, but don't go wild. A simple container that does the job will suffice. Remember, it's the product you're selling, not the container. Let the product speak for itself. The shipping label often provides a place to identify the company and do a little advertising. Of course, if the shipping box will be used by the customer for storing the product, some identification, perhaps on the side, is practical. Some companies feel the container is all important; in the limited edition plate field it's a popular belief. But I didn't happen to feel that way, and after all, by the time the customer gets the product, there's already been a money commitment . . . the product sold itself. This is not to say use a crummy container, but use one with simple lines that look smart. It can be classy and plain at the same time.

As you make your decision about what to ship your product in, remember that the weight of the container plays a big part in the cost. Popular containers are made of corrugated material, baskets, woven material, and styrofoam. As we discussed in Chapter Two, weight at the post office or shipper will make the difference in your shipping cost and profit margin. So it stands to reason to look around for the lightest, strongest shippers.

Containers fit different needs. Corrugated boxes I found, were not beneficial to me in the plate business. The styrofoam shipper costs a few pennies more but there was no further expense from breakage or remanufacturing. The product arrived in one piece. On the other hand, a good strong corrugated box is great to ship fruit, books, and non-breakables in. I also found a styrofoam shipper to be stronger with less weight and when you're trying to get a plate, shipper, and insert card with the customer's label under 16 oz. (if you are non-profit), you guessed it—styrofoam was the answer. A friend, Fred Simon of Omaha Steaks, uses styrofoam for his products because he uses dry ice and the shipper will maintain his product frozen until delivery and he has the added bonus of lighter weight for the shipping cost. Take all these considerations under study and you'll save bucks and get your product there in better condition than if you make a snap judgement about containers. Find a box company that will measure your product and make a size for you that will allow your product to fit into it easily but travel snugly. Made-to-order corrugated boxes, even in small amounts, are fairly inexpensive.

Unfortunately when one's in business one does experience returns. This is another reason to have strong containers to protect your product. A container has to make two trips. With your guarantee you will have returns. You will have to repackage the product, but if it has been shipped in a good firm container in the first place, you will have a damage-free product to ship to another customer. Of course, most foods and a few other products are non-returnable. If you market these products, you'll have to allow for some losses when you figure your expenses.

Now you have it: the product on one hand, the shipping container on the other. Be sure they're compatible. By that I mean be sure you can get your product into the container. Oh, come on, you say. Yet I've seen this costly mistake made over and over. So try the product inside a trial container as soon as you get the two together. Once that is checked out, you will have to decide on the best way to seal the container. There are several methods but three popular ones are staples, heavy sticky tape, or glue. Some shippers used to tie their containers together with string, but that doesn't look very professional. Be sure your product's container portrays quality, warmth, and simplicity that will draw your customer inside to the product, the star of this whole show, the minute the package arrives on your customer's doorstep.

Chapter 7

BUILDING A BUSINESS RELATIONSHIP
Keeping the Customer

As you get into selling, you will run across a few characters unique to your business. But there are some general types that all mail order businesses encounter. As long as you deliver what you say you will, Hilda Happy will stick with you through thick and thin. She is tickled with your product, you, and your company. A group of Hildas become your business family. They buy from you year after year. It is important that you find little perks to reward them so their interest stays up. One company I deal with does this by a bonus point program. After I acquire so many points I get special goodies. It usually gets me to buy more just so I can get better perks. Am I hooked, or am I hooked?!

Then there's Michael J. Mad. Remember what it took you to get this customer! For heaven's sake, don't argue with him on the phone. Let Michael vent his anger. Sometimes, there's no recourse but to say, "I'm sorry the product didn't work out for you," and cheerfully give Mike his money back. On the other hand, especially if the item is food, you might turn Michael Mad around by saying, "Look, just keep the item as a gift from us with our best wishes. Maybe we can try to serve you another time. We're sorry our product wasn't what you wanted." I realize if it's an expensive item, you can't do that, but at least do what you can. Go have the item picked up and send Michael his refund as quickly as possible. Sometimes Michael J. is so taken back by your cooperativeness that he will be an ambassador for your company from then on.

Impulsive Irma keeps calling you and changing her order. Be patient. As long as she keeps adding items to her order, so what? Unfortunately, sometimes she decides she doesn't want as much as she originally ordered. Irma's file will look like hen scratch. More fun . . . she keeps you guessing.

Complaining Carlos can drive you crazy. There is no way you can please C.C. He really wants the product, but somehow it is never quite right. It should be more round, the color should be red, not black, etc. etc. etc. I encountered this type endlessly in the collectible china business. In one series there was a rim of 24K gold. Complaining Carlos and a myriad of his brothers found invisible chips in plates to be replaced, or that the gold rim wasn't wide enough, etc. These customers take lots of patience, but remember how hard it was to get them. Keep smiling.

A special type of customer is Fred Friend. Sweet old Freds ingratiate themselves into your life. They wonder what they can do to help you. They call every morning to make sure you are still there. They give you suggestions on how to improve your product. I must say they come up with some really innovative ideas. I found I used more than one of these ideas through the years. I love Fred Friends, especially for being so interested in helping the business be a success. The problem with this Fred is that he has dedicated his life to talking on the phone to you. Well, don't get in a hurry; take the time because he is one mainstay of your business. Oftentimes these calls are the only outside communication Fred has so be a little charitable. Fred or Fredette may be elderly, shut-in, or just plain lonely.

Bad Debt Betty really doesn't mean to defraud you: it just works out that way. Sometimes she has something terrible happen to her after she has ordered the product. Her social security check didn't come and she can't get to the post office to send the product back. Some B.D.B.'s move away after they receive the product and amazingly enough forget to pay the bill. But, there are a few Bettys out there that make a practice of ordering everything they can with no intention of paying the bill. I have found that after eight collection letters and a phone call, collection is next to impossible. In a few cases, if you spread Betty's pay-out over several payments, you will get some money and she will stay with you. However, if all else fails, you must send the unpaid invoices to a collection agency. The agencies will charge you 25% for a period of six months with 50% after that. Use them. Remember, it is your money you're trying to collect. So anything you can get will help your bottom line. In checking new orders, be sure to check your bad debt list to make sure Betty isn't on it. If she is, put Betty's order in File 13.

About 25 years ago my husband Frank, who's been in the mail order business all his life, was asked to come to New York to testify in a mail fraud case. I wish you could have seen the piles of products the court wheeled in as evidence. These guys had made a business of ripping off mail order businesses. Even with the proof in hand, and on the courtroom floor, these fellows got a 2-year probated sentence. And do you know after the case was settled, it was revealed that these fellows had been tried two times before without conviction! Thank goodness, there isn't much of that kind of bad business practice out there. But as careful as you will become, you will still have some bad debt.

Since we've pretty well covered the types of customers you will be dealing with, let's talk about the types of correspondence you will be getting from them and what kinds you will be sending to them:

From the customer:
1. The Inquiry—"Please send more advertising information."
2. Delivery Problems—"Product hasn't arrived—where is it?" "My product is damaged—what do I do?" "I sent a gift to a dear friend. I haven't heard from them. Can you tell me if it arrived or not?"
3. Payments

From you
1. Check bounces
2. Credit card information
3. Notification of credit
4. Incomplete check
5. Change of address
6. Refunds

Customers need to correspond and this correspondence needs to be answered. You will find that most of your correspondence will fit the nine categories above plus a few that will have to do with your product. Do yourself a favor and put together a set of form letters. There are several examples for you to draw from at the end of this chapter. Not every letter you write has to be original. In fact, that would be an expensive use of your time. Draft a letter that will fit most of your types of correspondence. If the letter needs a bit of other information, add it at the bottom by hand or typewriter. The nice thing about the form letter is that it can be printed ahead of time. Only the name of the customer need be added, plus the president's signature. People feel more comfortable about their correspondence if a president of a firm uses his signature. If you have a computer, you can print out the correct letter when you need it.

Be sure your correspondence is handled in a timely manner. Don't stack it up for weeks. Try to have your answers back in the mail the following day or so. When the mail comes, date each piece, then divide the mail into the different work categories—payments, orders, requests, and so on. After this, dive right in and get on the typewriter or on the phone.

The telephone in the office. What types are there? How can you use it to your best advantage?

Building a Business Relationship

First, the types of long-distance systems are endless, from A T & T to Sprint. Remember your telephone is one of the most important instruments you have in your office so be sure it works. For several months I used two types of systems to see if one really could beat A T & T. Because our group seemed to be long-winded and we took a long time with our customers, the non-A T & T didn't win. Test your phone practices to see what system works best for you. The most important uses of the phone will be the free 800 number for your incoming calls. The type of phone system that will handle your 800 number is called in-watts, people calling your firm. You did remember to put it in your advertising piece, didn't you? Then you will be wanting to use an out-watts line for the United States and perhaps an out-watts line in your state. Again you will have to check to see if it pays against regular service. One advantage of using out-watts as opposed to regular telephone service is that the lines can be set up on a rotary system so while one line is engaged in conversation another line will ring. The beauty also is it's just one telephone number. Another advantage is in many cases out-watts will charge your firm a flat fee for so many hours of calling. That way you can call as many people as you want for that given time span. The process works in the same way for an in-watts. Some businesses use the 900 number on their advertising but that isn't free and it surely can make a customer mad. Don't do it. Use the 800 free, friendly number. Along with your phone system get an answering machine. When you can't be there, it is a wonderful tool. Say something as simple as

"This is Mary with Tribute. Our office hours are from 8 a.m. until 5 p.m. Monday through Friday. Please leave your name and telephone number where you can be reached, and the time you would like us to call you back."

Answering devices can be fixed for different lengths of messages. Try to give your customer as much time as they need to reply. Often, they can say everything you need to know in less time than that.

Sometimes they will even leave their credit card information on the recorder and don't want to be called back. A telephone answering device greatly extends your customer service. With the United States waking up at different hours, no customer need be frustrated by his one chance to make a call if you give him the chance to contact you on his own time.

Taking orders by phone means those warm calls we talked about earlier. Below is a form that shows you what to ask while taking orders on your incoming calls. Be sure your voice is happy. Make a practice of smiling when the phone rings. It should be a natural response—after all, the sound of the bell means $$, AND, you can hardly answer in a grumpy tone of voice when you have just smiled. The smile comes over the telephone line.

"Good morning, this is TRIBUTE. How may I help you? (pause. They will begin to tell you why they have called. Respond after every sentence or two.) Would you please give me your name, address and telephone number with the area code first. (Sometimes this takes a little time. Ask to have names spelled for you.) How will you want to pay for your order, VISA, MASTER CARD OR AMERICAN EXPRESS? (Wait for the answer "Yes", "I see," "Oh", "Really?", "That's good", "I'm sorry"—what ever fits.) Would you please read me the charge number. (Pause) Now would you give me the expiration date and what name is listed on the card. (Pause) Let's see if I have all this written correctly? (Read all the information back to the customer). I will be happy now to take your order. (Write all information down and then . . .) Please let me go over the order with you again to make sure it is the way you want it and to make sure that no one is accidentally left out of your gift list. You can rest assured I will process your order today and that your gifts will arrive at the appropriate times. We appreciate your business and our company is happy to have you as a new customer and friend. I will keep your information on file, so if you think of anything else you would like to order, just call me . . . my name is _____ and I'll be happy to take care of you. (Pause) Thank You for calling!"

When you talk on the phone, I suggest that you keep a mirror in front of you to maintain a cheerful voice. The telephone company offers a little program on the proper use of telephone manners for your employees. Take advantage of it. There's no turn-off worse than "What did you say?" A grouchy order-taker, talking too fast, or too slow—what a way to lose customers! Do yourself a favor: make absolutely sure your employees who answer the phone are professionals at it, yourself included.

After you have finished the call, be sure to make a note of the call, what it was about, the date, and what resolution took place. Then file the note.

These are not cold calls. These are warm calls, and the customer really appreciates it when he/she is treated like an old friend. Stroke your customers by giving them your name. When they call back from time to time, they will ask for you. Oftentimes, companies want to let the customer know how big they are. They instruct their telephone people to be as impersonal as possible. Mistake! In most instances, customers like to feel they are dealing with other humans. They dislike the idea that they might be giving business to a mega-corporation run by automatons. They pay better too if they think you are small. So no matter how large you grow, stay small, warm and friendly to your customer over the phone.

Probably the most important thing you do in an office besides get your money deposited is handle your orders. Be sure you know where your orders are at all times. This may seem like a funny admonition but before you can get them processed, a customer may call in and ask what they ordered or want to change the credit card he/she is going to use. What can you do? The phone is ringing off the wall with orders, and you haven't had time to divide them into 10 zips yet, or get them filed. At this point, you need an emergency filing system for incoming orders. The simplest way to do this is to make a 3×5 card for each order as it comes in, noting on there the customer's name, zip code, method of payment, and date you received the order. Keep these cards filed alphabetically in a box near your phone. You can't believe how fast you can whip out an answer. If there is a change as a result of the phone call, make the change on the 3×5 card and attach it to the order when you find it. Hopefully, you have put the orders in wire baskets by days received. It is good to keep these 3×5 cards until you can have the information up on a computer. If you can't have a computer, keep the 3×5 cards close to you at all times. The customer's names with the zip code will get you into your files in a fast and orderly manner.

FORM LETTERS

These form letters are a guide in helping you in your office day to day.
Use them in good health and prosperity.

Thank you for your inquiry asking for additional advertising
material. I hope the enclosures will help you. Please write or
give us a call if we can be of further assistance.

Your friend,

Name of President

Thank you for taking time to let us hear from you.

We always want you to be pleased with each plate you receive
from our office. If any plate is less than perfect, we can have it
replaced.

Please return your plate to our office by UPS or Parcel Post
insured, and we will gladly reimburse you for your postage.

We are sorry for this inconvenience, and will be looking forward
to hearing from you.

Sincerely,

Marilyn Schultz

Thank you for taking time to let us hear from you.

We always want you to be pleased with each plate you receive from our office. If any plate is less than perfect, we can have it remade with your old registration number. The old plate will be smashed. Since the plate is hand made, please allow eight weeks to fashion your new plate.

Return your defective plate to us by UPS or Parcel Post insured, and we will gladly reimburse you for your postage.

We will be looking forward to hearing from you.

Sincerely,

Marilyn Schultz

Your last Letter Writers plate was already on its way to you when you asked to have your order cancelled. No further plates will be sent.

Should you not wish to keep this last plate, just return it to our office by UPS or Parcel Post insured. As soon as we receive the plate back in the office, we will cancel and credit your account.

If we can be of further service, do not hesitate to contact us.

Sincerely,

Marilyn Schultz

Oops! We need a signature on your check.

Enclosed is a reply envelope.

We appreciate your continuing friendship.

Sincerely,

Marilyn Schultz

Thank you for taking time to inform us that you have returned the _____ . However, we have not received it in our office, yet.

Please provide us with information on how the plate was returned, or check with your local post office. Perhaps, they can help locate it.

We appreciate your cooperation in this matter, and we will be looking forward to hearing from you soon. For your convenience, please use our toll-free number (1-800-531-7469).

Sincerely,

Marilyn Schultz

Dear Collector,

We were recently notified by the U.S. Postal Service that you have changed your address. Before we actually make this change on our account records, would you please verify that the following address is correct:

Please return this letter indicating the accuracy of this change or, if you prefer, use our toll free number (800-531-7469). It is most important that we receive this information so that future shipments can be handled properly.

Thank you in advance for your cooperation. We look forward to continue serving you in the future.

Sincerely,

Marilyn Schultz

Account #

Thank you for taking time to let us hear from you.

Please find enclosed a copy of the Negative Option Plan letter announcing your new series. The Negative Option Plan explains in detail that if you do not respond by a given time your order goes into full production. The plate is then made and fired just for *you*.

Being a member of the Museum gives you the exclusive right to examine the plate in the privacy of your own home. Live with it and enjoy it for two weeks—then if you do not wish to keep it— notify the Museum. We will mail you a plate return label. Send the plate back and all charges will be removed.

If we can be of further assistance please let us know.

Sincerely,

Marilyn Schultz

We are writing in regard to a shipment of the LAVENDER LACE demitasse cup and saucer set.

Since you do not wish to keep this demitasse set, please find enclosed a label for use in returning it to our office for cancellation. It is not necessary for you to pay any postage when you use this label.

Just follow these simple instructions:
1. Prepare the package containing the merchandise for reshipment.
2. Moisten the back of the label and place it on the package.
3. Mail the package at any post office or in any mail deposit receptacle.

If we can be of any further assistance let us know.

Sincerely,

Marilyn Schultz

As you have asked no further demitasse sets will be sent to you.

Enclosed is the invoice for the last set shipped to you. Just put your check in the enclosed envelope and we'll be all square and even.

Thank you for your continuing friendship.

Sincerely,

Marilyn Schultz

Thank you for letting us hear from you.

You have an unquestioned 6 month buy back guarantee. On any plates you have purchased during the last 6 months, just return them and we'll immediately send you a refund of your full purchase price.

On older plates, you may wish to advertise them in the classified section of:

The Plate Collector Magazine
P.O. Box 1729
San Marcos, TX 78667

Such an ad doesn't cost much. Your continued friendship is most appreciated.

Cordially,

Marilyn Schultz

Chapter 8

SHIPPING
You Must Deliver

Halfway through. It's time for a little relaxation technique. You'll find by using this once or twice a day you will have an easier time finding answers for your business problems. This method allows answers to pop into your head more easily. To start with find a comfortable chair or just lean back in your desk chair, take a deep breath and picture if you will warm weather, an island in the sun, rays beating down on the water. The clear blue water around you is glistening and wraps around you like a warm blanket. There are sail boards, shrimp boats and lots of colorful coral and white sand. Swimming lazily around your ankles are little brightly colored fish. You have a tall cool drink and as you stand there, you are aware of swaying palm trees in the gentle breeze. Your mind can't concentrate on anything but this picture. Drift into this mental vacation for a few minutes, then take a couple of deep long breaths, coming up slowly. While you're in this relaxed state, maybe it has helped you to decide whether or not to ship your product yourself.

Chapter Six talks about the different ways to get your product to the customer, but we didn't discuss what procedures and paper work you will need to follow to get that product to the customer. There are three types of shipping possible for your product: 1) you will both warehouse and ship the product, 2) customer orders will be filled from several different sites, or 3) your product will be shipped from one site by someone other than you.

In any of the three shipping methods you will still be responsible for your customer's order that has to be registered into a shipping record of some kind. You will still be responsible for arranging for your product, its container, the product and customer inventory control, the shipping labels and anything else to do with the entire package such as package inserts advertising. I agree, there's a lot to do, and seemingly all at once.

But when you begin to go through the procedure step by step, it will become manageable.

Inventory is the name of the process of keeping an itemized list or catalog of goods that come into an office. Inventory control then means keeping a continuous record by either adding to or taking away from what has been shipped from the inventory.

Warehousing in general is comprised of the product being delivered to and stored at your office site. The number of items you will be selling will determine the number of charts you will need to keep track of. Even if you are having your product or products drop-shipped you will want a weekly copy of the firm's inventory transaction.

When the product or products are delivered to the warehouse site, the first thing you will want to do is count every box and its contents, check the product against the manifest of the truck driver that has delivered it, and then against your purchase order to make sure the product delivery is correct. If at all possible, check the product for damage while the driver is there. That's not really a reality because most drivers make you sign for the product before they leave, and they don't have much delivery time, but if you can stall them long enough—do it. Once you have checked the product for correct count and damage, you will want to record what you have received. If you keep a daily tally sheet of what comes into the office site, the inventory is easier to keep up with. To show you how easy it can be I provide an example for you in Chapter Seventeen. Keep the tally sheets on a handy clipboard. The main thing is to always have it at the same location. At the end of the month, transfer the information to a master sheet so you will have the information for the monthly report. Now, hopefully, what comes in must go out. RIGHT!!!

So how do you do it? In Chapter Fourteen we will discuss putting the customer's name, address and other pertinent information in some kind of filing and keeping system. But for now what you need to know for this chapter is that when you are ready to make your first shipment, have that list in one hand, and your shipping labels in the other. If any special advertising piece or package stuffer is to be put in, those as well. A package stuffer might be many different things. You may want to tell more about your product. You may want to put another order blank inside in hopes your customer, when he/she sees how great the product is, will want to buy more. A popular insert is "Do you have a friend?" and in some cases, you may want to advertise another business's product that doesn't compete with yours. The charge to the other company can run anywhere from $45 a thousand to $100 a thousand. This is a popular sales technique. You may want to try your advertising in some other business's product package as well.

Shipping

The master list—the record of your inventory—now becomes your shipping record. As the correct product leaves your place, you will need to mark the shipping record in the following ways:

1. the date it is shipped
2. the shipping agent (UPS, Postal Service, etc.)
3. the amount of the shipment
4. how much inventory is left

By keeping this data, you can determine the answers to any number of other questions.

How much do you still expect to be shipped? Do you need to reorder at this time? Do you need to do additional marketing? If you have an employee shipping for you or have the product drop-shipped by a fulfillment house, you will need to obtain this information. Make two more copies, one for your bookkeeper, and one for THE BOSS. In fact, you may be both, plus the shipping employee, but it is still a good idea to have three copies. Keep one in each file: Boss, Bookkeeper, Shipping.

Now that you know how to bring the product in and ship it out the door, which means of shipping are you going to use? Is your product only meant to be shipped inside your state—intrastate, or from one state to the next—interstate, or both? In Texas many years United Parcel Service (UPS) was not allowed to ship within the state. But they could ship to all other states. Where china was concerned, we had to find another carrier who could ship within the state. So we used Parcel Post and Tex Pack. What I'm trying to point out is that you may have to use a variety of methods to get your product to the customer.

For shipping fruit, the best and fastest way is by the post office. Because of their weight, books are best shipped by UPS or a similar type carrier. If on the other hand you only have one book to ship then you can't beat fourth class at the post office. Have a look around, for the quickest delivery time and cheapest shipping cost. If you have a perishable product, you may have to pay a bit more to have your product arrive in a fresh and timely manner. Be sure the customer knows the trouble you've gone to for him. SERVICE!!!

Well, hasn't this been fun? But just as what goes up must come down, so some products that go out must come back.

Hopefully, you have done your homework well and sent a first class product. But it seems sometimes that no matter what, the customer decides he just doesn't want the product after all or it arrives damaged. Sometimes a customer will just send the product back on his own, but in other cases you will have two options. The UPS procedure is for you to call them so they will respond with a "call tag" to that customer. This means that UPS will only pick up the item that you have requested. You do not have to mail anything to the customer. If the customer wants more than the specified item picked up he/she will have to make that request through your office. UPS will not pick up more than the items your office has cleared for pickup. UPS then will deliver the merchandise back to you. After you've got it, register the return on a return tally sheet. With the return you will also have to credit the customer paid in full. The other method of return is by the post office and it is called "return receipt requested". You will need to send the tag to the customer for him to affix to the package. Then he drops it in the mail. The same procedure above goes into action when the item comes back to you.

After you have checked for product damage and credited the customer, you will need to repackage the item for resale. If there is damage to the product, your charge includes insurance and UPS will pay you for the damage. If you take post office insurance on the product you will be reimbursed as well: however the post office insurance is an additional cost. An explanation of this type of insurance may be found in Chapter Eighteen. It is so much cheaper and you don't need to add this additional cost to the product and to the customer.

My experience was that very few things shipped by the post office ever had to be replaced. Most did arrive, and in fine shape too.

But when wild and crazy things do happen occasionally, they are usually worth the loss for the laugh they provide you and your workers. For instance, you know that if a customer isn't at home, UPS may leave the package with a neighbor. One of our customers called us six months after we replaced a plate to say that the lost plate had been found. For some reason UPS had put the plate on the customer's back porch slightly under the wood pile, or so the customer said, to avoid its being stolen. What can I say? One neighbor thought her friend next door was sending her rose plate gifts. The friend worked, so UPS continued to leave the plate at the neighbor's. I'm afraid the neighbors were no longer "friendly".

It is true that if you are drop-shipping, these are some one else's headaches, or are they? If you have a company do this function for you, be well advised it's going to cost plenty. However, if you check it against what it would cost for you to do all of the above, maybe it will be cheaper just to do the marketing and let someone else do the fulfillment. Only you can decide. Anyway you go, your dream—your product—will now be out in the world. Can you believe it???

Chapter 9

COLLECTING YOUR $$$
Finally!

Money, Webster says, is something of value such as gold, silver, or copper, stamped by government authority and used as a medium of exchange. That's the work exchange. You want to exchange your product for money —so that you can exchange it for something else like food or entertainment. That's why you work. That's why you decided to go into the direct marketing business. Now, it is time to get your $$$.

Several methods of payment will be apparent to you as you begin receiving orders. Some of your customers will send a check ahead to pay for the product. Several will have given you their credit card number. Some will want credit until they see the product—these are called open-billing. For these customers, an invoice is placed on top of the box of your product that is shipped and many will pay their charges from this procedure, as shown below.

This invoice covers your newest plate in the All-America Rose Series. Your collector's plate has been made of finest china using an original painting by artist Luther Bookout. You are assured of receiving the same plate number on each plate as long as you have accepted the previously issued plate.

To charge to your credit card, give card number on back of form.
INVOICE FOR THIS SHIPMENT ONLY

ACCOUNT NUMBER	DATE	AMOUNT DUE	
○ 115586843 000	11/15/	49 00	PLEASE PAY THIS AMOUNT

RETURN TO

THE AMERICAN ROSE SOCIETY
1006 South Tenth
McAllen, Texas 78501

PLATE	NUMBER
MARINA	6843

MS. HELEN CUSTOMER
123 ELM STREET
ANYTOWN, USA 00000

RETURN THIS INVOICE WITH PAYMENT TO INSURE PROPER IDENTIFICATION

(Back of invoice)

Please charge my plates to my credit card:

☐ American Express ☐ Visa ☐ Master Charge

Card Number_____Expiration Date_____

Signature _____

Please return this invoice promptly to

The American Rose Society
1006 South Tenth
McAllen, Texas 78501

As you can see, all sorts of things can be on the invoice. In the example provided you can see a bit of advertising goes along with it as well. Then you have their account number and amount due. If the customer has already paid by credit card the amount due would show "0".

As one always trying to convert my cash customers into credit card customers, on the back of the invoice I give them a second chance to use their credit card.

Also on the invoice the account number is translated to be the zip code, in this case the plate number and the last three 000 if they had any recipients. This easy customer account number makes life easy. If you want to, you can also place their original key number from the list they came from—just another step in customer tracking. Not every business will have a plate number so be creative and add something specific to your product in that slot. If you are sending a certain pack out, then use that number. There are many ways to make up an account number, but remember not to mess with the first five digits—that's their zip code and the basis for the zip-code-last-name method. So hands off those five.

Some will not pay from the invoice you have provided them and you will have to begin the collection procedure that is outlined in Chapter Seventeen.

As you see above, you will have three types of payments 1) cash 2) credit card 3) open-billing. Cash is usually sent in by check. Sprinkled among this group will be some actual cash and perhaps a few money orders. These cash sales will probably represent 1/4 to 1/3 of your actual money collected. Money orders are sometimes sent to you under this category as well. These money orders are usually for out-of-the-country sales —Canada, Europe, etc.

Credit cards are my favorite payment type, although any type of payment is fine with me! Though there are endless numbers and brands of credit cards out there, you will probably be accepting the three major ones —American Express, Visa and Mastercard. Even though you have to pay a fee to the credit card company on the gross sale it is worth it. Do shop around for as good a deal as you can find. The percent you are charged has to do with the volume of business that you do. So as you grow, keep checking to see if you can get lower rates. Credit cards will represent about 1/2 of all your business. Besides, it is convenient and easy for the customer to order from your company over the phone (FREE if you have an 800#) and it only takes five minutes to get all the customer information you need over the phone. People like telephoning in their orders too for the very fact that they can call back in for more products and they only have to give you their name and zip number. Be sure with the original call you explain to customers that you will keep all their information on file and confidential so they know that additional ordering won't take up much of their time. Review the telephone script in Chapter Seven.

People want service and remember, your customers are time-oriented. The beauty for you of their purchasing a product by Visa or Mastercard is that the moment you ship the customer the product, you can submit the charges to the bank, and you have your money on the spot with your percentage deducted. Let's sidestep here for a minute. Sometimes when a customer calls in wanting to have his product credited—that is, he wants a refund—you will submit the credit to the bank. If the credit doesn't show up the first month to the customer, he/she might call the bank and insist that the bank make the credit then and there. This is called a charge-back. The customer now has been credited two times. It can be a mess. It is best up front to talk to your credit card department at the bank and ask them to call you before they deduct any money to make sure you haven't already issued credit to that customer. AND . . . you make sure that when you do issue credit for that customer that you send the customer a letter telling them you have already issued credit and that it is possible it will take two billing cycles for the credit to show up on their credit card. You may save yourself an unhappy customer, save yourself a few grey hairs and keep from having a mad banker. *TAKE THE CREDIT CARD DEPARTMENT OUT TO LUNCH.* This charge-back service is not free. It can run as high as $45.00 for each transaction. Very costly, so watch out.

American Express is different in that their pay schedule takes three weeks before you are paid. On the other hand, you don't have charge-back problems. American Express won't issue credit until you give the authorization. No double dipping here.

The third type of payment is called open billing. Open billing really means the customer doesn't have to pay for the item he's purchased until he sees it. In other words, you have extended them credit. The customers then send in a check or call in their credit card number. Using this marketing method can readily insure a higher number of orders, but your bad debts can eat you up if you're not careful. I was very fortunate in my business that my bad debt ran around 2% overall. I hear horror stories of 10% and up. That just isn't necessary if you are watching what you're doing. That's not to say from time to time one project won't inspire an unusually large number of bad debts. Fortunately I didn't have many bad experiences. Learn from your mistakes.

There are several ways to protect yourself against large losses. If you have had the customer before and he has already paid by check, then he is probably a good risk. Credit cards are checked against a book that is put out monthly. If a name is not in the book the credit card is usually a good risk. If you have any doubts, you can call the bank and have the card checked out.

What if you want to try open billing on a cold mailing? Most firms give open billing on that first order. However, until you have more experience I caution you not to give this privilege out on your initial one or two mailings. Only after testing your original list to see how well the checks stood up would you want to consider doing it. Check to see that it is what I call an honest list. The list you rent must be clean. By that I mean well-maintained good addresses and up-to-date information. If you stumble into a bad list then you will have bad debt. This can happen if you don't rent through a good brokerage house but trade lists with another company. They mean to have had addresses checked, but they haven't gotten to it yet. Slow down and build a good business base before you issue open-billing.

Now we're going to talk about advance payments. In reality when a customer sends a check ahead of the shipment, that is what he is doing. On the other hand, some customers get confused as to whether or not they have already paid. Sometimes, you will receive two, maybe three checks. This is when you pick up that phone and call the customer. If you are in a continuation business, such as food, then you will ask them if they would like the check to go on the next item that will be coming their way. If yes, then mark it well in your shipping records and apply against the next shipment. If not, write a refund check.

When you first get your order into the house, be sure you write an acknowledgement card, a step we've talked about elsewhere in the book. I am providing you with an example on the following page. You will want to make variations and that's fine. Use this example as a guide.

SWEET AS SUGAR GROVES

3405 INTERNATIONAL BOULEVARD
BROWNSVILLE, TX 78521-3227
1-800-248-7872

Dear Customer,

Thank you for your order. You can rest assured that your order will be processed with all of our special care & attention. If we can be of any further assistance, please do not hesitate to call us.

Your friend,

Carl Samek

Carl Samek, President

Let me point out to you what needs to be in the acknowledgement:

1. receipt of the order.
2. date the product will be shipped if a date or "will be shipped as you requested" hasn't been mentioned in the original advertising.
3. your telephone number
4. address.

For the acknowledgement, I like to use a $3^{1}/_{2} \times 5$ postcard on a continuous form: however, I have used letters as well. So use anything you want to use, but be sure you use it. With some products when you send an acknowledgement in letter form, you may want to include a certificate. Some items are special and the certificate will show authenticity. If it is a limited edition or a numbered edition, then it would show these specifics. The possibilities are endless.

When you get your money, put it in the bank pronto. You will need a bank deposit book, the proper credit card machines and paper, and a record of your deposits. Here is where bookkeeping is all important. Most of these things you can really do yourself. The forms have been provided for you in Chapter Seventeen. However, I have added a daily tally sheet that is a wonderful backup for all of your transactions. In Chapter Seventeen are the monthly report form and your daily deposit form. The daily report form is just another thing you can do to keep up every day until the monthly report is prepared. The monthly report will tell what you have done last month, the record of deposits will tell you what you did today, and this tally sheet will tell you where you are going.

Below is an example of a daily sheet. Insert the names of your products where mine are now listed.

The daily tally sheet in this case shows the plate name that the company represents. For your use—perhaps you're shipping socks, different books, or clothes—write each name in a separate column as I have done here for individual issues. As your product is shipped, enter it right away on this tally sheet. Put down the gross amount of money owed. When the payments come in each day, put them down and deduct them from the total. Be sure you don't forget to put the gross amount of the credit cards down, not the net. Then the combined total paid each day of all your products. The following column will be your accounts receivable to date. Then be sure you enter your cancels, and you will have some charge-offs, (debts you or your collection agency can't collect), your prepayments (those advanced payments we talked about), and how much money is tied up in collections at your collection agency. (I want to give credit to a great collection firm that I use, Winston and Sherman of New York. They really do a splendid job for me, being very businesslike and collecting most of what I couldn't collect myself.)

With this daily tally sheet I could look in a moment's notice and see what I had outstanding. This is the kind of detail you need to keep up with so nothing gets out of hand. Sometimes a red flag goes up and you can jump on it immediately.

One thing I forgot to mention about depositing your checks is that there is a little brass plate you can have sent to your bank that has all your deposit information on it. It fits on their computer set-up so the bank does the fill-in-the-blanks instead of you. This will save you from having to turn that check over and write "For Deposit Only" on it and all the business information that the bank needs to deposit the check. The cost is minimal: however, most people don't know about it. As you grow, it will save your employees time and the bother of having to endorse checks. So get them to order it for you.

ITEM I	$	$	ITEM II	$	TOTAL SHIPMENT	TOTAL $	OTHERS	TOTAL PAYMENTS & CANCELS	ACCOUNTS RECEIVABLE TO DATE	CHG. OFF	PRE-PAYMENTS	COLLECTION AGENCY

Chapter 10

IN-HOUSE FINANCES
Keeping up with Your $

Keeping up with your money may sound difficult but it's not. I have found people try to make things more difficult than they actually are. It is true that there is a lot of paper work in the direct marketing business, but the paper consists of just a few forms done in large amounts. In Chapter Sixteen I will give you a breakdown on the responsibilities of other members of the office but in this chapter we are just going to talk about money and bookkeepers.

When you think about money, you may immediately think book-keeper, the money person of the firm. And you're right. Money is the duty of the bookkeeper and yourself. In fact, you may represent both. Money will include payroll, credit return, marketing your money, the payables to the company, the banking, the monthly reports, using the chart of accounts, and going to see the accountant. It may seem awesome. Don't throw up your hands! Let's take it one item at a time.

PAYROLL: Even if you are running your business alone, you will need to pay yourself. It is a good idea to set an appointed day, such as a Thursday, to do that, the reason being it is a good idea to get in the habit of paying yourself something or the next thing you know, you haven't taken any money out of the business and you find you are working for nothing. Sure, you say, I have just sunk everything into this project and there isn't any money to pay myself. You can start by paying yourself a small salary and setting aside a little money towards your loan. Before you know it you will have your loan paid off. If you wait and try to do it all at once it will seem monumental.

If you are paying employees, Thursday is a good day to do payroll. That way you can give the checks out on Friday. So many employers wait until their employees finish work on Friday to start figuring up the wages for the week. If you close out the books on Thursday, the checks can be done the first thing Friday morning and handed out to the employees at lunch time so that they can do their banking before the Friday afternoon bank rush. Your employees will love you for that.

Go out and buy a payroll form book. I have enclosed a page from one I have to show you what you will need to do each week.

On the payroll example sheet you will notice that you will figure first the gross earnings. This will be what you are paying your employee by the hour times the number of hours he/she has worked during the week. Then you will deduct social security, withholding tax, insurance, or any other special deduction you have agreed on. For a while, several of my girls wanted to have savings accounts so we deducted that as well and deposited their money to their savings accounts at the bank. What you will be left with is called Net Pay. When you are filling in the payroll checks be sure you list these deductions so the employee will know what his actual gross pay is. One more thing you might put on this sheet is whether or not the employee is married or single and how many deductions he/she has. Each year, social security and withholding amounts change so you will have to get an updated form from IRS. But again, this payroll form, as you can see, is not difficult.

One more thing you or a bookkeeper can do in the money department is keep a petty cash box. Every company needs one, at home or in the office. You can't believe all the little items that require a dollar or two. My bookkeeper had a real deal going—the coke machine. We all paid in and any little bit of money that she got from that would be used to have a company party. We got enough money to have a birthday party each April —meat tray, potato salad, etc. Lots of fun. Her petty cash box also sold stamps when an employee needed one. The possibilities are endless. Be sure you lock it up each night in a safe place.

CREDIT RETURNS: Writing a check to the customer for credit is a simple form of credit return. A bit more involved is crediting the credit cards. In Chapter Seventeen I give you detailed instructions on both of these and how they are done. But, there are other chores attached to credit returns besides cash and credit card adjustments. The product comes back into inventory. It has to be checked for damage and then put back out for sale. You will add it back into your inventory. Then you will have to re-market the item. Keeping track of credit returns can make or break you. They are all important.

MARKETING MONEY: This money I divorce from the actual fixed cost of running a business. This money is only earmarked for the actual marketing of your product. It is not to be added in to the other costs of doing business. Your marketing money will be used for your advertising piece, postage, and space ads or any other advertising medium that you might use. In Chapter Two I provided a money form so you will know what you need to get your advertising off the ground. I mention here cash flow. That's the amount of money you will need to function with. Cash flow includes marketing and fixed costs. Just remember that asking enough money from your lender can save you unneeded stress. Keep your pencil sharp. It really takes three years before you will breathe easily. Never let your guard down. Keep right on top of every dime. It's the dimes that can make you a success.

PAYABLES TO THE BUSINESS: Your role here will be getting the money collected for your product. No matter how well you plan a mailing that says "We take cash and credit cards," you get a customer that says, "I will pay by money order when I get the product." What do you do? Well, are you a gambler? Nine chances out of ten it's probably a good risk. If you never had this customer before and if the list hasn't been tested for honest pay, what do you have to go on? First, is it a friend of the company? Has your product been recommended by someone you have done business with? You really don't have much to go on. It's a calculated risk; I'd probably take it, especially if the order came over the phone. Somehow, phone orders seem more honest. Maybe the customer feels more responsible because he/she knows you really know who they are. The mail can be a bit more chancy. But after all, you have paid for the advertising piece and worked so hard to get these customers, it is worth taking the chance.

Another form of payables will be what you owe your suppliers. Now that's different. You will have to pay them too. Sometimes, that's not so easy. But if you can't pay all of the bill, at least pay something on it. And if you have planned your money needs well, you won't be in this spot.

BANKING: Each day you will want to take the monies collected to the bank. It's just a good idea to get them out of your home or office. Money lying around is too tempting. If you do the batching technique that is spelled out for you in Chapter Seventeen your time at the bank will be short. So many people just take their checks and hand them to the teller. What a bore! Time wasted! Your really don't know if she added them right, etc. Do it yourself. The tellers will catch on fast that you know what you are doing. That way your valuable time isn't wasted standing in line with twenty other merchants. The bank will give you a bag to put your checks in and when the money is deposited, you will receive a deposit slip.

Immediately mark the deposit into your check book if you haven't done it right before heading for the bank.

From time to time you will probably have to take your banker a financial statement demonstrating your business health. Be prepared to do just that. After all, he wants to make sure you are worth the credit he's advanced to you. So just say, "Sure, I'd be happy to bring my reports." Happy you, Happy banker.

MONTHLY REPORTS: A monthly report tells you what you actually did last month in your business. It also tells you what is still due the company —payables. Let me walk you through this example. On the cover page you will have the name of your company and the date of the month of your report. The front sheet, as you can see, is an excellent place to list your inventory. Inventory can slip up on you so this way you can see what you have all in one glance. You can see right away what you have to remarket. On the second page you can see what you have shipped this last month. Also on this page you will see if orders are cash sales—non-open billing, or if customers need to be sent an invoice—open billing. The third page reflects what you have sold in your inventory from last month. Under each item sold you will see what payments have been made during the month, what you need to charge off as bad debt, and what is still owed you from the original sale of each item. Sometimes you will even have people who paid ahead and the item hasn't been shipped yet. You must record these as well.

Now the page you really aren't thrilled about is what you have to turn over to your collection agency. You will have exhausted your collection procedure with the eight letters and a friendly phone call and you just don't have time or the staff to keep going after them. So you turn them over to the collection agency. Again I can't say enough for these great people. An outstanding balance of an item can start out being a huge amount and by the time they have done their magic an item can drop from $26,000.00 owed by difficult customers to perhaps $5,000 still outstanding. When that item's original gross was only $200,000 to start with, that can be the substantial profit you hoped for being recovered by the collection agency.

Next will be a record of your returns for the month and the returns value. The next part of the monthly report will be the actual deposit sheets immediately followed by a record of the credit card deposits. Lastly, you will have an accounting sheet of the actual money transactions for the month.

The monthly report may seem like a lot of trouble, but it is a tool whereby you will keep abreast of your business and will be able to keep on top of things easily.

CHART OF ACCOUNTS: You and/or your bookkeeper can mark the check stubs from this. I have placed one in this chapter for you. The chart of accounts is what your accountant will need to prepare your income tax and your financial reports from. Most bookkeepers aren't qualified to prepare these reports. The chart of accounts will classify each division of your spending habits, from bank charges (classified number 101) to taking a client to lunch number (125) including your employees' 1040's. As you can see, the chart of accounts covers everything from voided checks to your federal income tax expense. The numbers out to the side 100 through 941—are how you mark your bank stubs. These numbers are then recorded in the accountant's office and your reports are prepared.

As we observed earlier, an accountant is much more expensive than a bookkeeper. So do the everyday things yourself or use a bookkeeper in your firm. But send the big stuff to the accountant.

There you have it. In-house financing—the money. My final word of advice . . . Take it easy on wild spending from your account. Save your dollars for marketing for new customers.

COST CENTER	ACCOUNT MAJOR	SUB	DESCRIPTION
	100		VOIDED CHECKS
	103		CASH ON DEPOSIT-
	104		CASH ON DEPOSIT-
	105		CASH ON DEPOSIT-
	121		ACCOUNTS RECEIVABLE
	122		ACCOUNTS RECEIVABLE-EMPLOYEES
	123		ACCOUNTS RECEIVABLE-OFFICER'S
	124		ACCOUNTS RECEIVABLE-OTHER
	125		RETURNED CHECKS RECEIVABLE
	145		ESTIMATED TAX PAYMENTS
	161		INVENTORY
	169		INVENTORY INCREASE/DECREASE
	206		FURNITURE, FIXTURES, OFFICE, EQUIP.
	206	10	ARS
	206	20	MIM
	206	30	OFC
	207		ACCUM DEPR-FURN, FIXTS, OFC EQUIP.
	207	10	ARS
	207	20	MIM
	207	30	OFC
	207		TRANSPORTATION EQUIPMENT
	208		ACCUM DEPR-TRANS EQUIP
	209		
	210		MACHINERY AND EQUIPMENT
	211		ACCUM DEPR-MACH AND EQUIP.
	214		LEASEHOLD IMPROVEMENTS
	215		ACCUM DEPR-LEASEHOLD IMPR
	218		ORGANIZATION COSTS
	219		ACCUM AMORT-ORGANIZATION COSTS
	240		MEMBERSHIP CLUB
	295		SUSPENSE
	302		ACCOUNTS PAYABLE - TRADE
	321		FICA WITHHELD AND ACCRUED
	322		WITHHOLDING TAXES PAYABLE

COST CENTER	ACCOUNT MAJOR	SUB	DESCRIPTION
	323		TEC TAXES PAYABLE
	324		FUTA TAXES PAYABLE
	325		FICA AND WITHHOLDING DEPOSITS
	327		FUTA DEPOSITS
	341		FEDERAL INCOME TAXES PAYABLE
	371		DEFERRED INCOME
	410		NOTES PAYABLE TO
	411	10	NOTES PAYABLE
	411	11	
	411		
	411	20	
	411	31	NOTES PAYABLE
	412		
	432	10	
	432	13	
	432	21	
	413	11	NOTES PAYABLE - OFFICE
	413	20	
	413		
	413	21	LONG TERM NOTES PAYABLE
	414		CAPITAL STOCK
	501		
	502		CONTRIBUTED CAPITAL
	503		PAID IN CAPITAL
	504		TREASURY STOCK
	581	10	RETAINED EARNINGS
	581	20	ARS
	581		MIM
	581	30	OFC
	599		NET INCOME OR LOSS
	610		SALES - CASH FEES/SALES
	620		COMMISSIONS
	690		REFUNDS AND ALLOWANCES

COST CENTER	ACCOUNT MAJOR	SUB	DESCRIPTION
	701		COST GOODS SOLD
	702		FREIGHT IN
	703		DIRECT LABOR
	704		SUPPLIES
	709		OTHER DIRECT COSTS
	801		AD VALOREM TAXES
	802		ADVERTISING AND BUSINESS PROM
	804		AMORTIZATION
	806		AUTO AND TRUCK EXPENSE
	808		BAD DEBTS
	809		BANK CHARGES
	813		COFFEE BAR EXPENSES
	814		COMMISSIONS
	815		CONTRACT LABOR
	816		COMPUTER SERVICE
	817		CONSULTANT'S FEES
	818		CONTRIBUTIONS
	820		CREDIT AND COLLECTION EXPENSE
	820	10	
	820	10	
	824		DELIVERY
	826		DEPLETION
	830		DEPRECIATION
	832		DIRECTORS' FEES
	834		DUES AND SUBSCRIPTIONS
	836		ENTERTAINMENT
	842		FINANCE CHARGES
	844		FRANCHISE TAXES
	845		FREIGHT
	846		GAS OIL AND GREASE
	852		INSURANCE
	853		INSURANCE-GROUP
	858		INTEREST

COST CENTER	ACCOUNT MAJOR	SUB	DESCRIPTION
	853	10	JANITOR
	855	20	LAUNDRY AND LINEN
	855	30	LEGAL AND PROFESSIONAL
	856		LICENSES AND FEES
	858		OFFICE SUPPLIES
	860		PAYROLL TAX EXPENSE
	862		POSTAGE
	864		RENT
	868		RENT-EQUIPMENT
	869		REPAIRS AND MAINTENANCE
	870		RETIREMENT AND PROFIT SHARING
	871		SALARIES-OFFICERS
	872		SALARIES AND WAGES-OTHER
	874		SUPPLIES
	877		TELEPHONE AND TELEGRAPH
	878		TRAVEL
	882		UNIFORMS
	884		UTILITIES
	886		BAD DEBT RECOVERIES
	888		CASH OVER AND SHORT
	890		GAIN ON SALE OF FIXED ASSETS
	901		LOSS ON SALE OF FIXED ASSETS
	902		INTEREST INCOME
	908		MISCELLLANEOUS EXPENSE
	909		OTHER INCOME
	910		
	912		
	918		
	941		FEDERAL INCOME TAX EXPENSE

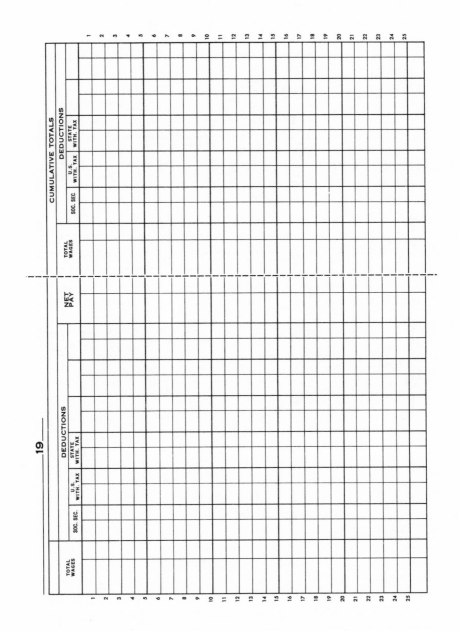

Mail Order on the Kitchen Table

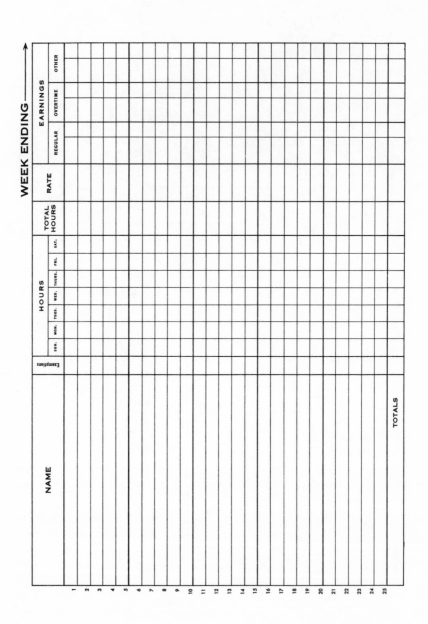

Chapter 11

BACK END ANALYZING
Holding Your Breath

I know you thought this day would never come. I compare the drop date—the day of your first mailing—to having a baby. It has been a long nine months to a year since the thought was conceived and now comes the actual delivery. I feel when the mail is finally dropped at the post office, it is a good time to take a little respite or trip. The post office says that once third-class bulk mail is dropped, it takes from seven to eighteen days before it is delivered through the postal mainstream. You should begin to get orders anywhere from seven days on. The work you have put in has been hard and laborious; you are tired. All you can do if you stay at home is wring your hands and worry. When will my mail start getting here? How many orders will I get? Get away and rest. It is important to you and to your business to be refreshed. So get away and relax for at least a week. I give you permission to do just that. If you decide not to take my advice you can expect long anxious hours while you sit by the phone and look blankly into the mail box. Take the trip. When you get back, your orders will have begun to trickle in.

ORDERS. Where will they all be coming from? Upon your return the orders will start coming in. Be sure to check the key number against your master list. This agony of anticipation can be almost unbearable. This is to insure you that all lists have been mailed. Many types of people will be buying from you. The orders will come from certain cross sections of people around the country. By studying what types of customers you have, you can focus your advertising. This procedure is called demographics. Demographics include learning the area of the United States and the world your orders come from, what economic class the customer belongs to, the age of the customer, how the customer pays, and as many other specifics as you want to know. There are companies whose specific purpose is to analyze customer lists. When you are mailing a small list and receive your orders, you can do these studies yourself. When I was mailing for The American Rose Society, I came to realize that although we received orders from all over the USA and abroad, the majority of the customers came from nine distinct areas. After discovering this fact the next reality was that orders were centered around rose and plate shows and famous rose-growing areas. The people who collected this series are older people—intellectuals, retirees, people with above-average incomes. Many grow rose gardens for a hobby. See what demographics are operative for your business. When you know things about your customers, you will know what type of list to rent in the future. That's one of the most important reasons for studying your customer's profile.

Two of my favorite customer stories that circulated around my company for years concerned customers of unusual demographic designation. One was a man who was confined to a wheel chair. He ordered every rose plate that was manufactured. But he never opened any of the boxes because he stored them immediately upon receipt. He didn't have any way to get to the basement where they were. After two years of steady ordering, he called one day to say how thrilled he was. An elevator had been put in from his floor of the building and he was now in the basement on the basement telephone calling us. He was so thrilled that he had his beautiful rose garden to enjoy. Not a dry eye in our office.

The other story is that of a customer who happened to go to prison in the midst of collecting his rose plate series. His checks started coming with a different signature and a different address. Our phone girls were hot on the phone to see why the address and signature were different but the man's name was the same as well as the plate number. Surprise! We found out that the signature was the warden's, and that the order was coming from a prison. He had been sent to jail for several years, for what reason we were never able to find out, but he was continuing to collect his rose plate series. We were sure he had the prettiest cell anywhere.

Another firm I was representing sold a series of Christmas stamp plates. Postmasters became a great part of the customer list. You begin to see what a cross section of interest and variety of people you get.

Not all the mail you will receive will be orders. You won't believe some of the stuff that comes in your postage paid envelopes. I didn't know a brick could be mailed in a #6 return envelope! Nor . . . that the post office would bill me $2.00 postage due, let alone accept that thing as a piece of mail. Sometimes just getting your mailing piece can turn a lot of religious freaks on. Your reply envelope will be filled with page after page of all sorts of religious papers. You have become their sounding board.

Then you have people who just want to be pen pals. My husband received a letter from Ghana, West Africa. The young man had seen our name on one of our shipping cartons. So he wrote my husband a letter. Can you believe it? How the carton got to West Africa we'll never know. The two of them have become true pen pals. Recently our mail man delivered my husband a pair of native thongs from Ghana made of nails and animal skins. And my husband sent calculators to the boys' high school class. You never know where your correspondence will lead you.

Now that the orders are on terra firma, how will you begin to read and interpret them? The first thing you will do is date the mail the minute it arrives in your office. Then you will divide the mail into three groups according to the indicated mode of payment: 1) cash 2) credit cards and 3) open-billing. Then take the key number from each card and place it on a yellow pad you have prepared. You may want a key number master sheet that you can tally at the end of each day with an individual yellow sheet for each individual list. There are several things you can record for each order—the list it came from, the key number for your house list, the number of orders for each customer from that list, the total amount the customer is spending, any gift items ordered. One of the reasons you check against your key code master list is to make sure that each list has been mailed.

Now, let's begin to analyze each order card. Take the ones with checks first, as they are the easiest to deal with. Make sure the amount of the check is the same as the customer's order. Sometimes, the customer can forget to add in any extra postage charges or other items. They don't mean to—it just happens. If the amount is incorrect, you will have to decide if the amount is worth calling the customer for or if on a reorder, you will bring it to his/her attention for the next purchase. If all the information on the check is correct, deposit the check in the bank. One nice thing about getting checks is that you can deposit them right away. This helps your long overdue dry spell for income. I suppose your checks will run about a third of your orders. Be sure you set up a file right away to show that customers have paid.

You will have received purchases by two types of credit card buyers —those by mail and those by telephone. The telephone orders you will have more control over, simply because you ask all the right questions and fill in the sheet in front of you while talking to the customer. I feel telephone orders are more secure. It seems people who call feel closer to your company and they feel more responsible about making sure their information is correct. For credit card mail orders, you will need to check to see if all the information on the card has been filled in.

With credit cards, you may, but should not put the charges into the bank until the actual day of product shipment. There are many good reasons you shouldn't anyway. More than once a customer will call back with credit card changes. Perhaps he's gone over the limit on one card and wants to change to another one. If the customer buys more products or wants fewer products, you just mark the change on his charge card and the 3×5 card you have at your desk. That way you won't worry about credit returns yet. While you are waiting to ship, go ahead and run the charge slips through your office machine. Then you will be ready to send the processed charges to the bank all in one batch at the same time you ship. It is really a nice, clean way to handle the charges. Somehow I feel it gives you more control. Be sure when you're checking the numbers on the cards that they have the right amount of numbers. Each card has a different length of numbers—MasterCard may have 13 or 16 members, and so forth. Also be sure the card has a signature. If it doesn't, a quick phone call to get the okay makes the customer feel more secure with your company. A phone call also provides a personal touch; the customer will know you're a caring company and it never hurts to be cautious.

Last, we will deal with open billing. Remember open billing is a request that the product be sent before payment is sent. It amounts to a charge account. When an order from your cold mailing comes through requesting open billing, there are some signals to help you decide if this is a good or bad order.

1. If the signature is in pencil and sloppy, set it aside. This doesn't mean it's a bad order but a neat ink signature is usually a sign of a good order. In this case, you'll have to use your intuition and perhaps assess the thrill you get out of gambling. Thirty-five years ago we received a large order written in sloppy pencil on a sheet of pulled out note book paper. This didn't mean it was a bad order, but it did signal to check the order a bit further. Call it insight or a gut feeling. Something said slow down, so a phone call to the town banker in Minnesota was in order. As it turned out, the call revealed that her husband was one of the largest baby food manufacturers in the nation. In fact, they had just given this little town a new hospital building. We made an immediate open billing shipment and she has been a good customer since.

2. Apartment house addresses and post office boxes instead of home addresses can be risky. I guess these people move around a lot, and they don't feel very responsible in making payments. This again doesn't mean that some aren't just fine.

3. Check the open billings to make sure they have a signature. These you should send back with a nice form letter asking for the signature. This will clean out a lot of bad orders. If you don't get a reply card back with a signature, you have lost the order, or have you?

You may have saved yourself the expense of the product. Of course, you surely hate to send an order card back, but if it is an honest customer they will be only too happy to sign it right away and return it.

Another reason for this is that kids will get hold of an order card and send it in for fun without the parents knowing anything about it.

Next let's take a look at list response. In Chapter Two, I gave you the formula's list response levels. You will receive all sorts of response. If you have had a previous house list, your response can be anywhere from 60% of the house list to 90%. On each cold list you will run from .002 to .01 and possibly higher, if it is a hot item. So don't try to figure out what a list will do until at least 10 working days into the project. List response will depend on your mailing piece and the list you have rented. You will just have to stick it out and wait to see if you did all the right homework. Sometimes, screwy things can happen: you mailed during a presidential voting week, or when a major war broke out in the Persian Gulf or during Super Bowl week. But it really takes as long as six weeks before you will have most of your orders in. Some orders may not come for years—it happened to me! Several years after a mailing had gone out, someone found the order card and sent it in. So hang in there.

I am going to give you a little formula that will show you what you might end up with. This formula is one I perfected over fifteen years, and it really works. It will get you into the ball park of where you will land at the end of the six-week period. First, get a calendar that you can keep close to your desk; an 8×10 size is good. When you receive the first order, mark that day one. Keep close track for four working days by marking the mailing results on the calendar each day. Now the second part of the formula is to begin again marking your calendar day one on the fifth working day since your first order came in. Keep all mail and telephone orders for the next seven working days. At the end of that period, add up the number of sales, both phone and mail orders, and multiply by two. Then go back and add in the orders you received the first four working days. This will give you more or less the amount of orders you will receive from your advertising. It is amazing how close you will come in your order response. The formula is simple and easy and will help relieve some of your stress about how you will come in at the finish line.

You now have your first house list. This house list will be how you make your living. Be sure you have all the customer information correct. At the end of your season, or product period, before the continuation mailing, you will want all this information in order to make wise decisions about your subsequent marketing techniques—your back end marketing effort.

Chapter 12

KEEP IT UP
Continuation Mailing and Back End Marketing

Five to six weeks after your first cold mailing your key codes will begin to take final shape as far as seeing how the mailing list is functioning. You really won't have all your orders in the house to work with for at least 3 to 4 months. But at least you will have a handle on the solid trends. If you had planned to make a roll-out mailing or a continuation mailing as soon as possible after your first cold mailing, then three months is a safe bet. I wouldn't suggest trying to mail any sooner. Why, you ask? There's just too much to do. Don't forget that any earlier, your mailing hasn't really settled down. When you remail will also depend on the product you are selling.

Before we go any further, let's elaborate on what a roll-out or continuation mailing is. Remailing to your original list after you applied the roll-out math is called a roll-out or continuation mailing. In other words you are continuing with the list selection you used on your original cold mailing—no new list. If you'll remember, when you were planning your original cold mailing, you planned your list selections with a good list broker. You will now need to give this person a call and alert him to when you want to remail and what list you will be using. As far as your printing and mailing house are concerned, if you liked their work, you'll need to give them a call to pencil you in just like you did for your original mailing. Follow all directions, as you did when preparing for the first mailing; after all, you are old hat at this now, except this time you may be mailing a much larger amount of mail.

I am going to illustrate a complete cold mailing in chart form. The orders you receive from the cold mailing will be called your official house list. Of course, all names are fictitious.

Let's say you are in the food business. The list you selected and mailed out was to food buyers. This then is the result of the mailing. In mail order language, response is discussed in per thousands. To arrive at per thousand mailed you divide the number 5.085 by 51 which is the number of orders you received from that list. You will notice that a period was placed after the first number. Now if you want to work in hundreds which is per cent (%) you place the period after the second number—50.85 divided by your response as shown below.

KEY CODE	NAME OF COMPANY	NAMES ORDERED	NAMES MAILED	ORDERS RECEIVED	ORDERS RECEIVED PER THOUSAND	ORDERS RECEIVED PER HUNDRED
0001	Schultz's Farms	5000	4999	33	6.6	.66
0002	Gallery of Nuts	5000	5001	27	5.4	.54
0003	Cheese Slices Inc.	5000	5085	51	10.0	1.00
0004	Food Magazine Esq.	5000	4090	3.27	.7	.07
0005	Fruit Cakes Divino	5000	4975	3.48	.7	.69
0006	Flip Flop Wines	5000	5000	.5	.1	.10
0007	Gourmet Emporium	5000	5150	6	1.0	.12
0008	Seafood City Inc.	5000	5003	22	4.5	.43
0009	Uptown Dept. Store	5000	4898	7.3	1.5	.14
0010	King Grapefruit	5000	5000	37	7.5	.74

O.K. there you have your results, what now??? To change the .74 hundredth into % you would say the result is 7 tenths of one per cent.

What does this all mean? Let's see which lists brought you the best results. Remember back in Chapter Two when you worked the sheet called "Results for a Profitable Mailing"? It told you how many customers you have to get to break even. Go back now and check to see how close the response level matches up.

In any mailing you will find maybe 4 or 5 lists that worked well for you and if you are a bit lucky, more. So don't be discouraged if you have 5 good lists and 5 not-so-rewarding lists. Let's pretend you have 5 lists to use towards your continuation or roll-out mailing: This is not to say that you can't mail the remaining list; it simply means that those lists will cost you more per thousand to get an order.

The aim of the continuation mailing is to get as many orders per thousand as cheaply as you can. The way you do that is to use the lists that gave you the highest response from the cold mailing.

.0045 Seafood City Inc.
.0054 Gallery of Nuts
.0066 Schultz's Farm
.0075 King Grapefruit Corp.
.0100 Cheese Slices Inc.

The next step is to restudy the information on the data cards that you received from your list broker about these 5 lists. One of the items you will be looking for on these cards is the size of their mailing list and the price per thousand to rent. Depending on what you are willing to settle for, go for the higher responses if you have a large enough universe, that is, available names a business owns that are mailable. If you have only 3 good lists and 2 so-so lists you'll have to decide if it's worth the mailing cost to get fewer orders. Sometimes it can be, especially if the company that you've received a smaller response from has a large universe and the 3 better lists have smaller universes. But back to our 5 good lists. Each has a universe of 30,000 to 1,000,000 names available for your continuation mailing.

Don't get in a hurry now. You must still hold back and take the mailing into the second step or phrase. For your second mailing (roll-out or continuation mailing), you can plan to mail five times your original list order. Each of the five lists were 5000 names more or less. When you ordered 5000 names from each company, (somehow it is rarely the exact number), you went through a merge purge. Your mailing came out somewhere around the actual number.

Let's say with your five good lists, you select five times the original 5000 names you mailed. Five times 5000 will yield 25,000 names from the company lists you are renting. So your continuation mailing will consist of 125,000 names. If you mailed 25,000 names in the beginning cold mailing and your response showed two good lists then you'd mail 50,000 names and so on. Your new response should reflect approximately the same number of orders as your first mailing did. If indeed it does, and it should, you are now in control. One of the things that occurs with a merge purge is that all names that are duplicated can be put into another mailing list, "The Dupe List" or "Multi-Buyer List". If you originally mailed 100,000 names, you might end up with 1500 names from that group that have bought items from several of the companies that you have rented names from—thus giving them these names. Their names are exceptionally good risks in mailing to a second time. They are known mail order buyers and they buy-buy-buy... From this point on you will more or less be able to forecast your response level for your business with confidence.

From the above scenario you see what to do for your first roll-out mailing. What if you want to do a third or fourth mailing or more? Some of the experts say use the same 5 × formula. Just to make sure, and still keep control, perhaps try an additional 25,000 names again. And if you're mailing in the smaller numbers, follow the same method as you did for your first roll-out mailing. I know it's slower going but your response is under control. Along with a continuation mailing it is a good idea to test 20% to 25% of your new mailing with cold lists. This way you may find a hidden knight to mail to next time. If your list has only 30,000 names on it then go ahead and use all the names on your third continuation.

So there you have it. Keep the new customers coming, but only where you have the control. You don't need instinct here: you need to follow your numbers. Don't gamble! Put your money on a sure thing—controlled list response!!!

So far in this chapter we have covered the continuation or roll-out mailing. I am now going to give you some additional hints on the back end marketing of your business. Back end marketing also is the method of keeping your existing customers by supplying them products on a regular basis. For example, you may be selling books to your customers. They have purchased the first of the series: now you must market the rest of the books in the series to them. Let's say there are five books in the series. Perhaps in your original advertising piece you may have spelled it out: there will be five books in the series with one book being shipped approximately every three months. This method of marketing is called automatic shipments. You automatically send the product to the customer without marketing each time and he pays you each time. If at any time the customer wants to cancel their account you accept that graciously and that's the end of the shipment; of course they have paid for what they have kept. So you have given your customer 15 days, 30 days, 6 months or 1 year to return merchandise. The customer's method of payments—open-billing, cash, or credit card—will determine when the actual shipment of book two in the series takes place. In other words, the customer doesn't get book two until he/she has paid for book one. And don't forget not everyone who bought the first book in the series will want to keep it. In fact, the hardest sell is the second in any series. It seems once the second item is purchased most customers will take the complete set of a series.

When purchasing inventory, take this into account. You really won't know the number of returns until your first shipment. So what do you do to get the first book purchaser to keep books one, two and three and so on, and pay for them in a timely manner?

Here's a tip or two:

1. When you ship book one, put a package stuffer in the box reminding the customer there are four more books coming in the series to come;

2. Use an incentive premium; after book three offer a FREE book-case to store the series in;

3. Offer to send the next four books at one time so the customer can read the series at leisure and only have to send one check or be charged one time;

4. Place a certificate of authenticity in the box. Books can also be collectibles. Only a certain number produced, or only a certain number produced within a specified time period. Certificates should give details about the product, (if it's limited, what its number is, the date it was produced).

Certificates can be used with almost any category of products. Note the example here:

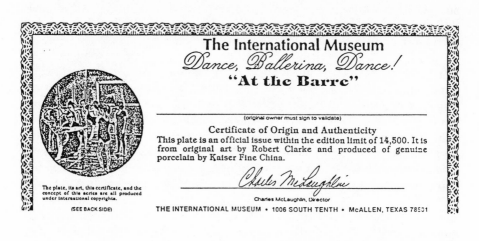

People like to know you are taking good care of them. The direct marketing business is a people business so stroke your customers.

You will, as you begin to know your customers, learn of other ways to keep your customers in a buying mood. That's great, you say, but my series is coming to a close. What do I do to stay in business? If you're lucky enough to have a food product like our family did for years, it sold itself. People will eat some kind of fruit each day. On the other hand, if you're not into edible products, you will be looking to bigger and better series or reorder items. One of our dear friends sells hunting gear. Have you ever known anyone interested in that hobby that wasn't constantly look-ing for something new? If you can keep supplying the existing customer over and over with products, you won't have the constant start-up cold mailing costs. Decide on how much of your product you want to sell. Then try to reach that goal in stages. After you reach your first goal, you may want to take a breather from the constant strain of mailing large blocks of names and just use fill-in marketing. This way you get a chance to catch up with the cash flow and the stability of your business. You don't have to do this but it is a suggestion.

The fine folks at Heritage House send a survey out to their existing customers testing three to five new ideas. When the survey comes back the interest will be rated accordingly as to which will be a good new possible series. You might try the same. Based on the response you can present a new series to the customer. One way to check to see about a new series is to call a cross section of your customers to see what they would be interested in. OR if you don't want to go that route, decide what you think will be a good new series and fly with it. More than one company has winged it this way and been successful. Have good marketing background experience before you give it a go and know what your customers are buying.

One important business vehicle to use with existing customers that won't cost you a lot of money is the negative option plan. This means they must reply only if they DON'T want the item in a series you are offering. Negative option is a fine and accepted method of direct marketing. It is often misunderstood or not used correctly. If it is used properly, it can be a valuable tool. When this method is used, it only requires a letter after the first sale, so your marketing is virtually cut to the bone. There is no return envelope required. Perhaps you will want to put a snapshot in the letter to your customer so that they can see the item. I call this the "NEGATIVE OPTION CLUB". Your customers will become members of this club. Over the years my customers really loved it. The important thing you must remember is that up front you must be clear to your customer that it is a club and it is a privilege to belong. They are valued and have a good credit history with your company.

This is the way it works...

The letter you write to your customer must give a number of stipulations. The rules are as set down in the Federal Trade Commission dated June 7, 1974. This ruling stands today. If you follow them exactly you will be within the law and you will enjoy using this marketing tool. Be sure you say:

1. If the customer does not wish to keep the product it can be returned;
2. The customer has no obligation to purchase a minimum quantity of merchandise;

3. The customer has the right to cancel his membership at any time;
4. The customer must be notified if he/she is paying for postage and handling;
5. The customer has 10 days to respond telling you he doesn't want to see this product, before you mail it to him for his inspection, after the negative option letter has been mailed;
6. If after the customer sees the product he doesn't want to keep it, he/she is guaranteed credit with the item returned;
7. The seller must provide return postage for the product;
8. The seller must let the customer know how often a product will be sent to him during the year for his viewing and possible acceptance.

Here is a negative option letter that you might use for a guide:

As you know, each year the United States Postal Service selects a Masterpiece Work of Fine Art for its annual Christmas stamp . . . . and our Museum is licensed to produce an on-going series of collector's plates using this stamp art. You have Botticelli's "Madonna and Child" from this past Christmas.

From time to time, the Postal Service also uses masterpiece art to celebrate special events. One of these "special events" was the honoring of the International Postal Union's 100th Anniversary. The art used for these extraordinarily beautiful stamps issued to celebrate this event is the work of such famous masters as Rubens, Gainsborough, and Raphael.

These works now will be incorporated into our *Masterpiece Art Series* of collector's plates. The first plate, this spring, is the historic portrait of Michelangelo by Raphael. Truly it is a rare opportunity for you the collector: a portrait of a famous artist by a famous artist.

I want you to see this *limited edition* plate in your own home. I want you to show it to your friends, to art lovers, to dealers.

So, unless I hear from you to the contrary, I will send you the portrait of Michelangelo plate as soon as it comes from the kiln. This plate will have your individual plate number—the same number as on your Christmas series—fired into its backstamp. Many collectors feel having a matched numbered set is most important.

After you receive this elegant, historic plate, inspect it carefully. Display it in your home for a full two weeks. You have this absolute and unquestioned right: if this work is not a prized addition to your collection, just return it. I'll immediately cancel the charge. You have the rare opportunity to see this first edition plate without risking a cent.

I'm anxious to have your opinion when you see Raphael's portrait of Michelangelo.

Now what must the customer do in your behalf? He must send the product back if he wants credit.

This marketing tool does have a larger rate of returns; however, you must plan for that. Sometimes it can be up to 50%. My suggestion here is to order a small quantity, test the negative option club response, and then order what else you will need. The returns can be shipped out to part of the list. That's one other nice thing about the club—wait for return response before shipping out to all your customers. The customers I had became used to the negative option club. They looked forward to seeing the product before they purchased it, previewing before the general public what new series was out. They got preferential treatment. They didn't have to waste time waiting for the mailing piece. It is with this attitude that you present the program. It stands to reason that not every customer likes the plan. You will have some disgruntled people that don't understand how the club works, but for those who do get the hang of it, you will find that you have a great sales technique working for you.

In any of your marketing—up front or back end—you must employ the 30-day rule. The 30-day rule simply means you must mail out your product when you say you will. If you can't get it out for one reason or another in 30 days after you said you would deliver then you must let your customer know. This is the law. Use a simple postcard saying why it can't be delivered and give the customer the right to cancel. You will get some negative response—that's just the breaks.

One other valuable back-end marketing tool is the telephone. Keep closely in touch with your customer. If you can answer by phone any paper correspondence that comes into your office you will establish that warm close tie with your customer.

No matter what your product is or how much you have going for you, keeping the back end up is where you'll make money, money, money by the buckets full.

Mail Order on the Kitchen Table

Heritage House Survey

Dear Subscriber:

I am writing you today to ask for your help—nothing more.

For several years we have been publishing beautiful, useful, reasonably priced books and collectibles for our subscribers. We were able to publish these products at such reasonable prices because friends like you have been kind enough to tell us in advance—through surveys like this—which of our ideas were of interest to them.

Recently we learned that many of our subscribers have an interest in collecting fine porcelain four-seasons plates and we now plan to issue one or more series and need your help in deciding which to publish first.

On the following pages we have pictured eight proposed designs for the four-seasons series. Would you help us by indicating those art concepts which appeal most to you? Of course, if none of them are appealing to you, please be frank and tell us so. But please keep in mind that the concept we issue will be produced in colors suitable for reproducing on fine porcelain.

It will take you only a few minutes to complete our questionnaire and return it in the self-addressed, postage-paid envelope we have provided. But I want to thank you now for helping us choose the ideas which will be most appreciated by our discriminating friends.

In order to complete this survey as soon as possible so we can commission artists and designers, we would appreciate your prompt reply. We have used your name and address merely for mailing purposes and your reply, of course, involves no commitment on your part.

Once again, we offer our sincere thanks for your help in this important survey. I can assure you it will help us bring you beautiful porcelain plates at the lowest prices possible.

Sincerely,

Keep It Up

How To Complete This Questionnaire

WE HAVE EIGHT PHOTOS OF DESIGNS WHICH HAVE BEEN PROPOSED FOR OUR FOUR-SEASONS PLATE SERIES. WOULD YOU BE KIND ENOUGH TO GIVE US SOME IDEA OF HOW APPEALING EACH DESIGN IS TO YOU? PLEASE CONSIDER EACH IDEA SEPARATELY AND MARK ONE SQUARE BESIDE EACH DESIGN TO INDICATE:

☐ I find this design very appealing.

☐ I find this design somewhat appealing.

☐ I find this design somewhat unappealing.

☐ I find this design somewhat unappealing.

PLEASE REMEMBER TO ANSWER THE FEW QUESTIONS ON THE BACK OF THIS SURVEY.

Title:	Wildflowers with poems
Concept:	A collection of wildflowers with a poem by famous poets such as Wordsworth, Shelly, etc.
____	I find this design very appealing.
____	I find this design somewhat appealing.
____	I find this design somewhat unappealing.
____	I find this design very unappealing.

Title:	Rustic Scenes
Concept:	A collection of rustic scenes such as milk cans, water pump, mail boxes, etc.
____	I find this design very appealing.
____	I find this design somewhat appealing.
____	I find this design somewhat unappealing.
____	I find this design very unappealing.

113

Mail Order on the Kitchen Table

About You and Your Family

Which idea described in this survey appeals to you most? _____

For the purposes of tabulation, kindly check the following as they relate to you and your family.

YOUR SEX: 1. ___ Male 2. ___ Female

YOUR APPROXIMATE AGE:

1. ___ Under 18   4. ___ 35–44

2. ___ 18–24   5. ___ 45–54

3. ___ 25–34   6. ___ 55 & over

ARE YOU: 1. ___ Married 2. ___ Single

YOUR HOBBIES:

1. ___ Cooking   5. ___ Travel

2. ___ Sewing   6. ___ Sports

3. ___ Crafts   7. ___ Reading

4. ___ Decorating

ARE THERE CHILDREN UNDER 18 LIVING IN YOUR HOUSEHOLD?

1. ___ Yes 2. ___ No

IF YES,

PLEASE CHECK THE AGES:

1. ___ Under 5

2. ___ 6–12

3. ___ 13–17

Please complete immediately and return in the enclosed postage paid envelope.
THANK YOU FOR YOUR HELP!

Heritage House Invitation for Membership

REPURCHASE GUARANTEE

THE AMERICAN ROSE SOCIETY agrees to purchase back your limited edition collector plate at any time within 12 months of delivery for your full purchase price, including postage and handling charges, provided it is in good condition. With this extraordinary risk-free guarantee, you should return this card and reserve your Cherished Roses of America collector plate today.

FOR FAST SERVICE,
CALL TOLL-FREE:

1·800·531·7469

IN TENNESSEE, 1·615·790·4256

THE AMERICAN ROSE SOCIETY
OFFICE OF RECORDS AND REGISTRATION

THIS IS A PRIVATE AND LIMITED INVITATION

*Please respond within ten days if you want to receive your **TWO FREE GIFTS**.*

Cherished Roses of America

The Award Winner Series

PREFERRED RESERVATION CARD

YES. I'll take advantage of your private invitation to me to take a no-risk look at "Voodoo" the first plate in *Cherished Roses of America,* the semi-annual series from the American Rose Society.

I understand that no money is due now, or until and unless I decide to keep "Voodoo." Two **free** gifts will accompany my plate, and **these are mine, regardless of what I decide to do.**

If I do decide to own "Voodoo," I owe nothing until 30 days after I have my plate. Then I pay my first installment of only $9.95. Three additional, convenient monthly installments of $9.95 each are due, until the entire purchase price of $37.95 + $1.85 shipping and insurance is paid. I understand I shall receive advance notice about the next semi-annual edition plate in *Cherished Roses of America,* the Award Winners series. **The two free gifts are mine, regardless.**

```
00108 014
ASAB7A03HX      000000000
H. H. SCHULTZ
100 N. TOWER
ALAMO, TX  78516                    CBJ
```

Please correct any errors in your name and address. We reserve the right to reject or cancel subscriptions at any time.

THE AMERICAN ROSE SOCIETY
P.O. Box 1408 • Nashville, TN 37202

114

Chapter 13

PITFALLS

Since you are studying and readying and analyzing, you might also do a little trouble-shooting. Let's see what Murphy can come up with. No matter how well you plan, or how hard you work, something simply CAN go wrong. If you plan for and are somewhat aware of these pitfalls, you can minimize your mistakes and cut out some of the surprise factor.

1) One of the commonest pitfalls is overdoing. In your enthusiasm to figure out how much product you will need, you may have a tendency to purchase way too much. In some cases you may be asked to place a minimum order just to get your product. A series of plates we were purchasing from Germany suggested we order a fixed number of plates #1 and #2. It was deemed necessary at that time because of the distance they had to come and we had the plan to ship plate #2 rather rapidly after plate one. The first plate number was fine, but it was almost a wild guess as to the stick rate—actual number of plates the customers would keep—on this particular subject matter. Most customers loved the first plate in the series, but weren't wild about the second, so, needless to say, we had plates coming out the kazoo. As it turned out we would have had plenty of time to have ordered #2 plate after #1. We would have saved ourselves from over- purchasing. Plates #3 to #6 in the series were well received. Ordering plates #3-#6 was a simple matter as we now had a good handle of how much inventory to purchase. It can happen to you. I think those #2 plates are still available if you want one! Learn from my mistake.

2) Another way of overloading is trying to sell too many items at the same time. Say you're so enamored with five products that you can't decide which one to sell first, so you try to sell all five. I believe this is called spreading yourself thin. Now if you are planning a catalogue and the items are related so that you can sell all five, that's okay. Then it's a planned expense. You just have five times as much invested.

3) This brings us to misfiguring. Things that can be misfigured are money, your timing and your customer response. A few years ago a dear friend, who shall remain nameless, did truly have a great idea. Unfortunately, the study into direct marketing response was not done, and this friend thought she'd get one order for every ten letters she mailed out. The mailing was a disaster. All her time, money, and effort just went down the drain. Oftentimes you hear of people buying a product they think people can't live without—and then they don't know how to market it, let alone how to purchase more product if their initial pitch should happen to work. Funny how they didn't think of that. A fine example of this is the guy who bought the Mexican shoes on the back side of the mountain in Acapulco for a steal and sold them like hot cakes. When he went back to purchase more shoes for his customers the craftsman was nowhere to be found. His business career I'm afraid was short lived.

4) Time is a hard one to grasp—the amount of time to get a mailing ready, the length of time to have your product produced, and on and on. Here you sit waiting for the special paper you want for a mailing and the paper mill runs out of *wood*. Think about it!!!

5) Then there's money mistakes. The old cash flow is stretched when customers take six months to pay for their product instead of the thirty days as you just knew they would. So think about this when you're planning your financial needs.

6) One hard one to plan for is phenomenal growth. A problem you say? But with growth it can mean a larger office or shipping space, more product, more personnel to handle the growth, much more money at a faster rate than you could have thought of in your wildest dreams. Don't lose control. Don't jump too fast. If it happens to you, don't let the business run away from you. You're running the business; it is not supposed to run you. If you're on top of every move in your business like you should be phenomenal growth might simply mean you go to prepared Plan B.

7) In our string of pitfalls one to mention is the slow mailing response. For some reason some mailings just get off to a slow start. That doesn't mean that your response level won't eventually get where you planned, but all you can do is sit and wait it out. I believe this is called grin and bear it. The formula I gave you in Chapter Eleven will work for what has come into the house those first 10 days, but if it's a slow mailing the orders may continue to dwindle in over the longer-than-expected six weeks to two-month time period one usually experiences. This will of course add additional orders you have been impatiently waiting to receive. One way to read your responses is to add them up each week and see if you're getting more or less the same amount of orders for several weeks without falling. Then once it begins to fall, see what the percentage is and

see how close it comes to the steady response. You can then figure if you need to do some additional marketing. I suggest Plan B and C and D to be in place in case this scenario happens to you. Don't rush into a wild campaign to try to get to the goal you have set for yourself. If you have several plans waiting in the wings, then you can put one into motion without losing all control and money. Back to an example on the steady response: Say you get 200 responses the first week, 240 the second week, 201 the third week, then dip to 150 responses the fourth week. Check the percentage drop. Analyze the trend. You can see the three weeks was a good slow but steady response—so if you've planned a 1000-order response by week four you have 791 towards your goal. You still have two or three more weeks of response and you're probably going to come very close to your goal. Sure, it would be nice if in three weeks you had the 1000 orders, but sometimes it just doesn't work that way. Be prepared!!!

8) Copy . . . Be sure your copy says what you mean it to say. At a recent convention, a friend of mine, Fred Simon from Omaha Steaks, had simply asked to have his tux sent ahead to the hotel from his office. For several hours the hotel looked for the clothing and finally tracked the suit down in the hotel freezer. The man at the hotel desk didn't read the label that had very explicit instructions on where the tux was to be delivered but instead he read the writing on the container which said "Keep Frozen". As hard as you try sometimes copy doesn't get understood the way you want it to.

9) Why is it that so many people who are in business think that if you're not growing, you're not successful? If that's not a mind set! Why put all that pressure on yourself? If you're happy selling 500 items and you can make the money you want at that price and you have easy control over your business—stay there. If you're not happy until you sell 25,000 units, then do that too. But don't fall into the trap of trying to grow just because somebody else thinks you should. Only do it if you have a good handle on the business and you have prepared for controlled growth, and only if you want to grow.

10) Be prepared to be sued, or to sue. No one ever wants this to happen, but you just can't be in business over the course of many years without it possibly coming to pass. So plan it as a possible business expense and keep good business records as you go along. That way you have solid back-up right at your fingertips when and if you need it.

11) There's the pitfall of not checking a calendar before you set your mail date. If you fail to check what's happening on a national level, a mailing can run into the wrong season for the product, a presidential campaign, holidays when people are thinking of other things, and the list goes on and on. A good example of this is when a company well known in the

117

industry mailed into Superbowl Sunday. I think you can imagine the response. *What* response is more like it. Thank goodness, that one pitfall never happened to me, but I had others, and so will you, but I also learned from other companies' mistakes. I'm sure you'll follow suit and do the same.

Chapter 14

DATA BASE FILING/COMPUTER USAGE
Keeping Records

Keeping records is perhaps the job most dreaded and thus most neglected in new businesses. It sometimes takes an income tax audit, a sales fumble, an irate customer, or a wrong bank accounting to make a record-keeping believer out of the direct marketing business person.

But painful hindsight doesn't have to be your teacher if you *make* yourself keep records correctly from the very beginning.

And you may not believe this but record-keeping can even be a turn-on! (Sure it is, you say.) As you are filing, train yourself to interpret the facts you are handling. Let your imagination drift to show you what might be done with this set of customers, that market projection. When you're filing bills, ask yourself if you should be getting bids on this or that item. Handling facts, figures, and names in record-keeping produces new ideas for making more money.

This chapter lays out some basic principles of direct marketing record-keeping. Don't skip it—either the chapter, or record-keeping.

Granted, record-keeping takes time and care, and much of what we keep, we never use again. So why do it? Simply because information is one of your most valuable assets. With this information, you will make your living. Your records are considered historical and legal. And you want them in a form so that you can pull out vital information instantly.

Let's clarify terms here. Because of the proliferation of computer technology, record-keeping is often called "data base management" today. A "data base" is simply a collection of facts about your house list arranged by categories for speedy retrieval, such as if the customer is a man or a woman, their age, the amount of money they have spent and so on. By extension, "data base" can be either facts stored in a computer or records kept in boxes or filing cabinets. Don't let the term "data base management" scare you. You were doing it when you were thirteen and rearranging your baseball cards on the floor of your bedroom after supper.

Another term that may need clarifying is "house list." This is your list of customers, the people you do business with. Your house list will be constantly augmented, mostly expanded as you get new customers from your mailings, and the information from their source keys as discussed in Chapter Four. A house list is defined as your customer list. These people have bought something from you. As you go along various people will request that they be sent a mailing, including friends and family, but until they buy something from you they are not in our house list. They are a potential customer. Once in a while you'll delete names from you active house list—bad debts or perhaps by special request. From your comprehensive house list come all your auxiliary lists, for example, a list of preferred customers or a list of customers in your immediate geographical range.

Now let's get on to your data base management.

Three types of stored information or data are vital to you:

1. **customer information:** sales transaction, profiles, data base, correspondence, etc.;
2. **current internal business information:** including bills, insurance, payroll, job descriptions, plans, bank loans, etc.;
3. **cumulative general business records:** daily print-outs, inventory, mailing records, etc.

Practically everything that comes into your office can be classified in one of the above three ways. You will need to make provisions early on to keep all three kinds of records, though of course you internal and cumulative business records will accrue more slowly than your customer transactions.

Set aside some time before your first orders come in to figure out the physical layout of your record system. You'll need some shelf space, a filing container, and an area where you can process your orders. If you don't have a filing cabinet, get an inexpensive accordion file from a local office supply company. Keep your equipment simple and inexpensive at first. As you begin to make money, you can invest in better and larger equipment, but for now, spend your money on getting customers. To help you think through your needs, here are three systems of filing necessary to the direct marketing business. You'll be using all three.

The first concerns what you do with your mail order responses when they come in. Record-keeping begins the minute you go to your post office box. (You see non-record-keepers standing in the lobby over the trash can, putting the important things under their arms and dropping envelopes with return addresses, notes, etc. in File 13.) To handle your orders, begin at the very outset using what is called the ZIP-CODE-LAST-NAME method. This is the type system adopted by the United States Post Office to insure rapid and correct delivery of your mailing piece. As you learn more about marketing, this filing method will become very clear to you and you'll see the advantages of using it. Even with a few customers, it's best to get into the habit—remember, you're hoping to be swamped with orders and you don't want to be changing filing systems in the middle of a land-office business!

The ZIP-CODE-LAST-NAME system means basically that you file orders first by the zip code and then by the last name of the customer. You are probably familiar generally with how zip codes are devised: the first three numbers designate a fairly large population area in a state; the last two narrow the piece of mail down to a small town or a section of a city; the additional four numbers added in recent years designate a post office box, apartment house, or block.

When you begin filing your orders, look on the address of the customer to determine the zip code. Put the lowest numbers first in the file, for example, "10017" before "78501". As you get more orders, you will need to look to the last two digits to tell which one goes first. Finally, if the zip codes are exactly the same, look at the last name of the customer and file alphabetically.

Presuming that you have lots of orders when you go to your post office box each day, you may want to get a sorting board for ease in sorting the mail. (See picture.) This handy piece of office equipment consists of

SORTING BOARD
(Tabletop View)

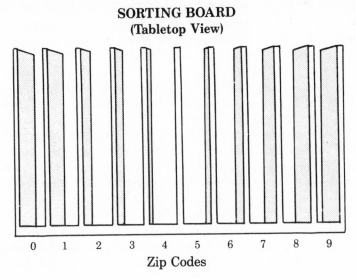

| 0 | 1 | 2 | 3 | 4 | 5 | 6 | 7 | 8 | 9 |

Zip Codes

ten slots, each slot holding a "000"- "100-", "200-" etc. designation for the first three numbers of zip code. After getting the mail arranged generally in these ten categories, go back to each slot and rearrange your orders by the last two digits, then by the last name of the customer. With the sorting board, if you are interrupted, you are never lost in your filing system. Your stacks await you. When you finish a stack, place a colored card or note on top of the pile stating it is in order. If you get busy and don't have time to file your mail after you've processed it, at least put a rubber band around your sorting board categories until you have time to file further.

You may ask at this point if this file of orders and correspondence is the house list. It is and it isn't. Think of it more as a cross-reference. You will need a "cleaner" list, that is, one more easily accessible such as a 3 × 5 card file of your customers' names or a list on your computer accessed by name, zip code, shipping or account number. This way, if a customer calls in with a question, you can get to the information quickly.

It is important to keep the 3 × 5 file for many reasons. Even when you have put all the information on a computer (I hope you can get one eventually) problems do happen. After being in business for four years and thinking we had all the data base on a wonderful computer program, a terrible thing happened. The computer program became overloaded and lost all our information. The computer man that I was using at the time hadn't made a copy of our customer list or the transactions and we had virtually nothing except our 3 × 5 cards remaining. It took us eight months and a new computer man (who understands making copies and keeping them in a safe place) to recover. This is an extreme case but it can happen. Keep at least a simple duplicate of your house list.

When you are ready to put the new orders or correspondence in your permanent file drawer, check these against what you already have in that zip code category. For example, do you already have a letter from Mr. Xanthia of 76205? If so, you'll need to clip Mr. Xanthia's new order *in front of* his letter.

The ZIP-CODE-LAST-NAME system really is so simple, yet it makes filing and record-keeping easy.

The second type of filing method is ALPHABETICAL BY SUBJECT OR NAME. You might use this method, for example, to cross- reference customers on 3 × 5 cards or on your computer as I mentioned in the paragraph above. If you use response cards to get customer information, these cards may be filed alphabetically by last name of the customer. They give you a wealth of information, such as how much the customer is willing to spend, what credit cards are used, and certain preferences in a product—in short, a whole array of information you need to increase the size of your business. And once you have these customers, you can mail to them over and over.

As your business grows, you may want to store information about customers in your computer. Good for you. Any number of pertinent facts can be placed on file so that you can draw up from this data base either the entire file on your customer, or, say, all the customers who live in New Jersey, or all who have ordered twice or more, or (very important for your cash flow!) all who are past due in their payments of accounts. Having this information at your fingertips is very helpful and will cut down time that you and your eventual employees have to spend going through the filing containers. But if the computer information isn't enough, then you have your files for back-up. And nothing can replace this wealth of information.

Alphabetical filing by subject is best for internal business records. No one has ever figured out anything much better than your basic manila folder, with the tab clearly marked for what's inside. Thus, you'll have a drawer in the file cabinet, or an expandable cardboard file, a wire basket or a cardboard box in which a folder marked "Electricity" will be followed by one called "Insurance" followed with one called "Loans," and so forth. Inside each folder some sort of order should be maintained, such as chronological placement by date for bills, or alphabetically by names for correspondence. Most people put the latest thing in the front of the folder. If you have information that goes together, paper-clip it rather than staple. However you organize, try to be consistent, making a few notes to yourself at first if you think you'll forget from one filing to the next how you've organized.

The other way to file is chronologically, by day, month, year—whatever fits what information you're wanting to save. In this category go such items as computer hard-copy print-out books of your records, your daily deposit sheets, and record books from freight carriers. This is where the shelf space comes in. Be sure you have plenty of space for saving.

And finally, a few random admonitions:

RESPECT YOUR FILES! Go to them over and over. Try to keep in mind what kinds of information you have painstakingly stored. Use your careful saving practices to your financial advantage when you are wondering whether to market a new product, what your accounts receivable are, how to tailor a product to the biggest geographical buying sector. This is called building a lifetime value history.

DON'T EVER THROW ANYTHING AWAY! Not cards, correspondence, complaints, or compliments. Stash everything. My first mailing taught me the hard way. Somehow an order card got lost—probably put in the garbage. Now that's bad enough, but this first mailing offered a prize of $1000 for the first order returned, and this particular card I knew was the first order! What was I going to do? Fortunately, the customer decided to order a second plate and called the next day. Was I ever quick to get all the information from her and thank my lucky stars! AND she got her $1000. It only took once to cure me. Let my experience do for you: when a piece of mail comes through the door, deal with it and then FILE IT.

FILING IS JUST PART OF RECORD-KEEPING. Let's make a distinction here. You file things you have on hand—cards, papers, bills, responses, flotsam and jetsam of all sorts. Record-keeping is a mindset, a mentality. Record-keeping is not just dealing with whatever comes your way in paper form. Record-keeping involves being aware of what you need a history on. With record-keeping you stay alert to all the potential information you may need. Thus, a phone conversation needs simple notes made about it—the date of the call, who called who about what, and the outcome of the conversation. That's record-keeping. When you put that note in the folder marked "Phone Calls", or with the other information you have with their zip you've filed something. A fine point? Not really. A record-keeping mind set is your ticket to efficiency, and it may well be your ticket to success in your new business.

During the chapter we have touched on computers. You can run a business without one and do it very well, but as soon as you can get one, do it. It will save you time and can give you so much information. Also as you grow, you won't be able to keep up with the physical work that it takes in a business to do it by hand. As soon as the manual work becomes too burdensome to handle, get a computer. Notice I said "get" one, not necessarily buy one. Many firms lease computer equipment; others will rent one to you for three years with a $1.00 sale at the end. There are many ways to get a computer without outrageous initial cost. I feel unless you want to deal with all the headaches of repairing equipment, having trouble with the programs, etc., that you're better off renting this service if your business becomes large. If your business is small then there are many wonderful computers that aren't expensive that you can use in your home. I might suggest on this level to purchase a home computer. Anyway you go, keep in mind that it's your record-keeping. Make it easy and convenient.

Chapter 15

YOUR OFFICE
Physical/Financial Considerations

After all you have gone through, this may be your most outrageous mental gymnastics: AN OFFICE. This is where you are actually going to do business. You are hanging out your shingle. Now you are seeing your business name come to life. It is a bit scary to realize at this point you can't turn back. Be comforted by knowing all your up-front work is getting ready to pay off. You are in business. Once you have gotten over your wet feet and sinking spell, you can pat yourself on the back. You've come a long way, baby!

Let's get physical! What size place is it going to take for you to run your business? By now you have already made your decision on who will fulfill your shipping. If you are going to do it yourself, then the question will really be how much room will it take for warehousing your product? If you are going to drop ship, as we discussed in Chapter Eight, then your space needs will be much smaller.

I have one set of good friends who works for a big cheese house. They decided they wanted to have a small mail order business from their home, candles. Remember how big they were in the 1960's? These people actually produced them in their basement and did the office work down there as well. They had a great deal of fun with the project and it didn't require much space for an office. Another friend ships books from one room of her house, while another room is used for her office.

When I began my plate business, I rented rooms from a company that didn't need the space at the time. It worked well for five years. We grew, they grew, and guess who had to move!

You have to have income to cover your office financial needs no matter where your business site is. If you start from your home it will be much cheaper and more easily accessible and practical. There are several benefits you can gain by working from your home. You can actually rent the office space from your existing home and take income tax deductions for utility bills, insurance, etc. But if you are in a position and have the money to start with a regular office outside your home, that's great too. One of my clients wanted, and could afford to start out with, a nice office. It was a labor of love putting it together. It really was a godsend to have it underway while waiting for the creative work to be done and the mail to be dropped. By the time the mailing was launched, my client's office was stocked and ready to go.

The most important thing when planning a work area is to make it easy to get to everything. For example, your telephone needs to be close to your files. Be sure the phone has a long cord so that while talking to your customer, you can be looking up their files. Customers hate to be put on hold. They also don't like to be called back—unless it really is a tough question and needs lots of time. So, make it a cheerful call by talking and looking up the file all at the same time. It's a little like patting your head and rubbing your stomach simultaneously.

I find that a square office is great. I have designed what I consider two perfect rooms that will work well for you.

You really can design your room any way that works best for you but remember that having your employees grouped together is important. You and/or your "manager" might be in different areas but having everyone else together makes it easier to operate. The manager and/or you need to be in sight of the group. The only employee who need not be in sight is your bookkeeper. That person needs lots of quiet. You might have a window or opening where you can see each other. I have found that when a customer calls in, someone in the room usually knows the problem and will know how to solve it. They can give you the work while you're chatting with your customer. If you are the only employee, then have everything close, easy and convenient to reach.

Since I sold my business, I keep my consulting office at home. It is true that my office laps over into my grown son's quarters, but this little-used space makes a great second room if I need extra help. Instead of having employees in the house, I farm out such projects as my bookkeeping. That way I don't have to pay payroll taxes and the like. I suggest you try to keep your overhead down by using the same method.

Now that you have decided on a work site, the amount of space needed, and how much help it is going to take, what equipment will you need? First, there will be the standard necessary items such as a typewriter, or computer and printer if possible, a copy machine, filing cabinets, sorting boards, adding machine, credit card machines, postage machine, stamping material and several sizes of wire baskets. Then come the common expendable supplies like rubber bands, paper clips, yellow

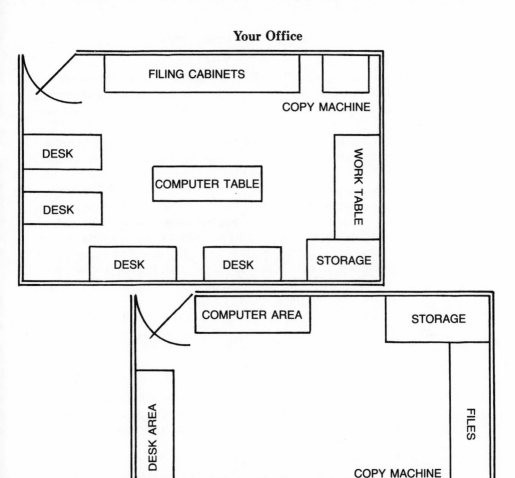

pads and pencils. Get several sizes of manila folders, pressure-sensitive labels to identify your folders, and bank deposit slips. Of course, you will want to purchase a few number six envelopes to send letters in. Then you will need a few number ten envelopes for use in paying your bills. You won't need much stationery, but you'll need some number six and number ten paper with your company name on it. These are standard sizes for responding to your customer because the paper is smaller and you won't have to say so much. Keep your message short, simple, and to the point. Also form letters and collection letters look nice on number six paper.

People don't feel they're in business unless they have a calling card. For a feeling of worth and a way to say, "I'm serious about my business," be sure to get a set of calling cards. Just get 500 at first. Be sure they are attractive and give the vital information about your firm, but avoid loading them with too much print. They tend to seem cheap and desperate if they look crowded. Don't let the printer sell you on thousands. Remember, you're mail order, not door to door, and won't be presenting your card and yourself to too many people. Spend this money getting customers.

Now one nice touch: You can either type them yourself or have them printed on continuous form post cards, but send "Thank you, Dear Customer, for your order" notes. Just keep the cards close to the typewriter and do a few each day. An example has been provided in Chapter Nine.

After deciding on your office equipment and supplies, it is furniture time. Don't go overboard here either. As great as it is to have new and beautiful furniture, spend the money getting customers. There are office furniture stores that have used furniture and filing cabinets—these will work well for your purpose now. When you make your first MIL, then get a new desk. One thing you must treat yourself to is a good chair. But again, there are great secondhand deals out there.

With the physical props in place, it is time to decide mundane things like office hours. Of course, if you're working out of the house, it might be catch-as-catch can. Maybe you will work hours while the kids are asleep or in school. If your spouse has to work nights, that makes a great time as well. If you have no home interruptions (My, aren't you special!), then any time will work. Whatever way works best for you, try to make your hours as regular as possible. A sloppy office system won't work. There have been many times for me that three in the morning has been an inspiring, quiet work time. If you actually have an office other than your home, then you're more tied into a regular office hour set-up.

The type of direct marketing product you will be selling may dictate your hours. One mail order camera repair business I have come into contact with doesn't open until 11:00 a.m. He does all his repairs in the morning and his return calls in the p.m. If your product is seasonal such as for Christmas, then your office hours may be fourteen to twenty-four hours daily for two or three months of the year. Some mail order businesses will require you to have regular office hours from 8 a.m. until 5 p.m. Perhaps you can only afford one or possibly two employees each day. Then spread your force out by having one work in the morning and one in the afternoon. There are special procedures in different parts of the day and having a certain employee handle these regularly works well. I always hated to open and close. You might want to make someone else take on that assignment. The point I'm trying to make is that you can cover a lot of time with very few people. Say, for instance, that you know when your mailing drops, you will be needing a few extra people to help answer the phone for a few days. Hire them just for that special time period.

There's no way around it; you will have some fixed costs such as the telephone, electricity, salaries, car and gasoline. By the way, the mileage rate for a contract worker who might be using his/her car to run your errands in recent years was 26c upwards a mile depending on the job and its location. Be vigilant about fixed costs. They have a way of getting away from you if you're not careful.

Chapter Fifteen has really been a quick but detailed overview of what you will need for your office. It is best to start out small and acquire more space as you grow. Don't be in a hurry but move into larger quarters when you just can't squeeze another item into what you now have. You will grow and need a larger office and more employees, which brings us to Chapter Sixteen: Personnel, Your Most Valuable Asset.

Chapter 16

PERSONNEL
Valuable Assets

Here are the people or jobs you will need to get the work done in your company. Perhaps at first, these thirteen people will all be you. As your operation expands, count on hiring someone to help you. If you are wildly successful, you may wind up with all thirteen jobs filled on a fulltime basis. This chapter is strictly nuts and bolts, with not much scintillating entertainment along the way. Cruise it on this, your initial read of the book, then remember where these details are for ready reference later on.

1. Owner
2. Direct Marketing Office Manager
3. Creative Marketing Manager (Account Executive)
4. Checks and Refund Cashier
5. Credit Card Cashier
6. General Clerk-Typist
7. Marketing Typist
8. Telephonist
9. Bookkeeper
10. Accountant
11. Shipping Clerk
12. Assistant Shipping Clerk
13. Office Runner

Below, I've dissected the various jobs to show specific responsibilities. You can use this information two ways: as a manual for employees, and as a realistic guide to the procedures needed to make your direct mail marketing firm work.

THE OWNER

You are responsible for all the jobs listed here that are required to make the company run! You the owner may do as many or as few of the functions as you need to financially or physically to insure your success. Much will depend on the size of your business operation. You will probably find you want to at least be knowledgeable about and in control of all operations. Even if you don't DO everything, know HOW to do everything. Hire any temporary help needed, using this manual to explain a specific task to the worker. Lucky Thirteen will soon become your number.

Specifically, as the owner, you

1. Are responsible for money to accomplish your project
2. Are legally responsible for your business
3. Set up your checking accounts
4. Establish good will with customers and employees
5. Furnish job descriptions for employees
6. Hire and fire
7. Provide employees with orientation handbook
8. Decide if you will have profit-sharing plan
9. Structure management so that office manager, bookkeeper, and marketing manager answer to you
10. Communicate with companies that supply your product.

DIRECT MARKETING OFFICE MANAGER

The direct marketing office manager is the first mate of your ship. He/she is your top assistant. Pick this person well and take plenty of time to train him/her. If you don't succeed with the first one, try again. Don't settle for just someone: the job will make or break you. You never know where your help will come from . A fine man who worked for me for years became ill, but the specialty work I was in made it almost impossible to find anyone to replace him locally. Feeling a bit down when the mail came, I found I was in store for a surprise. A man who had worked for many years with Book of the Month Club was wanting to relocate. It was an instant camaraderie. We both had a good deal and when the business was sold in 1985 he was affectionately taken into the new owner's fold. The direct marketing office manager should do the following:

1. Keep business running smoothly
2. Supervise employees after they are hired (In some cases you may designate office manager to hire)

3. See that all schedules are met
4. Function as backup for anyone who needs help in office
5. Read all outgoing correspondence
6. Order office supplies and stationery
7. See to maintenance of office machinery
8. Provide periodical financial reports

CREATIVE MARKETING MANAGER
(the account executive)

This person really has nothing to do with managing the office. His/her position is strictly marketing for the company. His work is up front with the actual acquiring of the customer and with the back end analyzing. The creative marketing manager does the following:

1. Does list planning and ordering
2. Is responsible for list analysis
3. Is in charge of telephone marketing
4. Orders product to be sold
5. Develops marketing plan and sets mailing dates
6. Supervises writing of copy for promotions
7. Places ads or promotions via media schedule
8. Is in charge of art work for mail piece
9. Is in charge of shipping label design, any additional marketing piece included in package, and art and copy for shipping container

CHECKS AND REFUNDS CASHIER

What a title! It almost sounds scary. Let's face it—there's power! The person who has their hands on the money better be trustworthy, and closed-mouthed outside of your business. He/she doesn't have a very glamorous position but this is one of the most important jobs you will have. Look at what he/she must do:

The checks and refunds cashier

1. Writes up the daily cash deposits
2. Writes up NSF deposits
3. Records the daily transactions into records system
4. Prepares statements

CREDIT CARD CASHIER

More money. It's all around you. The record keeping here is so different from that done by the checks and refunds cashier. This entails using the credit card machines and each has a different method of payment to your business. It is a different world. It certainly keeps one from getting bored.

The credit card cashier

1. Supervises credit card sales or payments, entering them into records system
2. Settles charge-backs
3. Writes up credit card deposits
4. Checks bank statements at end of month

GENERAL CLERK-TYPIST

The general clerk-typist covers a multitude of sins, things like filing for damages with the freight company when their truck runs over the shipping container with the product inside, (all the while the claims man standing there saying "Our truck didn't go over this," while the tire tracks are across it). It's the general clerk-typist's bright smile that wins UPS over for payment. Keep your general typist happy!

The general clerk-typist does the following:

1. Provides supplemental typing for overflow from marketing typist
2. Files and keeps records associated with business (not customer-related)
3. Files claim forms and receipts for shipping companies and United States Postal Service
4. Files shipping record forms from shipping companies and answers shipping correspondence
5. Calls for shipping company call tags and tracers
6. Does end-of-month postage billing
7. Compiles monthly shipping analysis for monthly report
8. Answers spill-over calls from telephonist
9. Types acknowledgements of orders, etc.

DIRECT MARKETING TYPIST

This person has one of the most fun positions in the firm. She/he really gets to know your customer. They become old friends. Mail is often addressed to this person. A customer feels he's getting personal attention here with a confidante to talk to. I have had many a late payment conscientiously finally made because my direct marketing typist sympathetically listened to the reasons the customer had gotten behind. (The "Better late than never" rule applied here). A good direct marketing typist is indispensable in keeping your business personalized to your customer's needs.

The direct marketing typist

1. Does filing and record-keeping of customers
2. Opens mail, dates it, takes key numbers off original orders
3. Checks to see if new order is already a customer
4. Corresponds with customers
5. Does all direct marketing typing
6. Does past-due account collection calling
7. Types donor-recipient cards and/or greeting cards

TELEPHONIST

This person keeps the line of communication open between the business and the customer. You'll want a cheerful soul for this position, or maybe you'll do this job yourself. You can answer all the questions asked and there will be many. The marketing telephonist can really have a lot of fun. Several years ago our firm thought it would be a good idea to call all of our existing customers to see how they like the product. We were also starting a new series and I felt it would be good to see what the customer wanted. This way they felt they were helping to plan the product. Putting our telephonist in charge, we brought in after office hours a group of women to make these phone calls. Dubbed instantly THE LADIES OF THE NIGHT, this group did a great job, we got all the information we wanted, and that season we had a healthy stick of customers.

The telephonist

1. Receives incoming calls
2. Does telephone marketing—if any
3. Takes messages off answering device and returns calls daily

BOOKKEEPER

The direct mail marketing business is definitely one with lots of paper work, record keeping and numbers. I suggest you choose a bookkeeper with confidentiality. AND give him/her a quiet place to work. No muzak!

The bookkeeper performs the following tasks:

1. Does monthly reports
2. Makes out payroll
3. Keeps track of work days, sick days, leaves, etc. of employees
4. Attempts collections of overdue customer accounts after normal mail and phone attempts are exhausted
5. Pays all bills connected with business—insurance, rent, etc.
6. Keeps petty cash box
7. Readies quarterly reports for accountant
8. Keeps daily record of all shipments

ACCOUNTANT

A bookkeeper, although very skilled in your everyday business accounts, can't do the elaborate work that an accountant does. Not many businesses can afford an accountant on a daily basis, but it's a good idea to try to get at least limited accounting services. Most accounting firms have programs on their computers that will take care of most of your needs and at a much faster rate. So here is a job you can't do. And you already have so much to do that it will be great to have someone check you for mistakes and omissions.

The accountant

1. Records all financial transactions of your business, checking for accuracy, irregularities, possible embezzlements, intercompany accounting etc.
2. Prepares your tax return
3. Aids you when you are audited
4. Prepares quarterly tax projections
5. Prepares the 1099's for your employees

SHIPPING CLERK

The warehouse man/woman has to be strong, have endurance, and care for the product. The shipping clerk needs to be able to sense when the product comes in wrong, broken or destroyed. It takes all these characteristics. We had a woman who was a great packer, but when she got through she had to call someone else to lift the box. She couldn't handle the weight. To the chagrin of all of us, we had to locate her elsewhere in the company. Watch for pitfalls of this nature when you're hiring a shipping clerk.

The shipping clerk

1. Is in charge of shipping
2. Takes inventory monthly of office supplies and sales products
3. Does office maintenance in slack shipping times
4. Is in charge of tally sheets each day; gives these to general clerk-typist for billing purposes on postage at end of month
5. Oversees product and shipping supplies to insure shipment at proper time
6. Runs inserting machine
7. Sees that postage is in meter
8. Records shipping transactions in record books

ASSISTANT SHIPPING CLERK

He/she is the right hand of the shipping clerk.
The assistant shipping clerk helps in the following ways:

1. Assists in warehousing and shipping of product
2. Assists in general housekeeping functions
3. Aids shipping clerk when duties reach overload

OFFICE RUNNER

This is not the person who runs the office but the one who runs to and from the office on errands. Though low in the hierarchy, this person is extremely important to the smooth functioning of an office. He/she must be completely trustworthy. The office runner

1. Does miscellaneous errands as needed
2. Takes money to the bank
3. Goes to the post office

EMPLOYEE ORIENTATION
HANDBOOK

_____

NAME

_____

POSITION

_____

DATE OF EMPLOYMENT

TABLE OF CONTENTS

TRIBUTE INC.

COMPENSATION SUMMARY
Fearless Schultz

Total Compensation per Hour Worked (based on 32 hours per week)	$ 6.67
Annual Salary (See Note A)	11,098.88
Insurance Premium (50%)	1,837.18
Profit Sharing Plan (Enter 5/1/80)	N/A
Longevity Bonus	300.00
TOTAL ANNUAL COMPENSATION	$ 13,236.06
TOTAL MONTHLY COMPENSATION	1,103.33
Annual Vacation (10 days)	.5mo
Annual Holidays (7 days)	.35mo
Total Months Worked	11.15
Total Compensation per Month Worked	$ 1,187.09

Note A The employer paid contribution to the Federal Social Security program relevant to your wage is $776.92.

INTRODUCTION

This handbook contains a statement of the basic facts, policies and procedures relevant to your employment. It is recommended that it be read thoroughly to acquaint yourself with the operation of the office and your role in it.

EMPLOYEE COMPENSATION

The following statements outline the principal components of the total compensation package associated with your employment.

A. Social Security Tax

Your employer makes a contribution in your behalf to the Federal Social Security program of an amount equal to the Social Security tax you pay. The annual contribution made relative to your employment is shown in the Compensation Summary.

B. Vacation

The basic vacation for employees is 2 weeks (10 working days) during the first thru 5th year. Vacation time during this period is earned on a monthly basis; 5/6 of a day for each month worked.

Following the 5th year of full-time employment vacation will be three (3) weeks (15 working days) per year earned at the rate of 1¼ days per month. A vacation day is based on the normal hours you work.

Each employee is expected to take vacation annually. No more than 15 vacation days can be accrued. A vacation schedule will be prepared annually in January by the Office Manager with consideration of the needs of the organization and the desires of the employees.

A new employee is not eligible to take vacation during the first six months of employment and no vacation pay is due upon termination during this period.

C. Holidays

This office observes the following paid holidays:

New Year's Day	Labor Day
Memorial Day	Thanksgiving Day
July Fourth	Christmas Day
Easter	

D. Health Insurance-Medical

A group medical and surgical insurance plan is available in conjunction with your employment. All full-time employees are eligible for coverage under this plan which is provided by Blue Cross-Blue Shield.

Your employer pays 50% of the premium for this coverage. The annual premium paid by your employer relevant to your coverage under this plan is shown in the compensation summary in this handbook.

Optional dependent coverage is available at group premium rates. No employer contribution is made for life insurance or cancer coverage.

E. Retirement and profit-sharing plan

Your employer provides a profit sharing plan administered by Happy Bank. Under this plan, your employer contributes from 0 to 15 percent of your annual wage.

All employees are eligible to participate in this plan. The employee's rights to your employer's contribution are 40% after four (4) years of employment and continue to increase at a rate of 10% per year until full vesting is earned after ten (10) years of employment. There is no cost to the employee to participate.

F. Bonus

A discretionary bonus may be distributed to all employees on May 31st. This bonus is given in recognition of the valuable contribution to the business success of the company and is in addition to the Profit-Sharing. To qualify, you must have been employed at least one year.

G. Overtime

While not anticipated, rarely overtime might be required. Hours worked in excess of forty hours per week will be compensated at one and one half times your usual hourly rate.

H. Pay Periods

Hourly employees are paid weekly on Friday afternoon for hours worked during the seven previous days.

I. Deductions

Government regulations require the following payroll deductions:
Social Security (F.I.C.A.)
Federal Income Tax

J. Salary and Performance Review

Salaries and performance of all personnel are reviewed annually, usually during the month of April.

PERSONNEL POLICIES

The following policies have been established as guides for employees.

A. Non Discrimination

This office will not discriminate against any employee or applicant for employment because of age, race, color, creed, sex, national origin, or marital status.

B. Confidentiality

Information concerning the nature, size and extent of business activities is confidential. Such information should not be discussed outside of the building or with individuals not directly involved.

C. Personal Appearance

Your appearance is important to our organization. You are expected to be dressed in suitable work clothes and be well groomed at all times.

D. Probationary Period

New salaried and full-time hourly employees are provided a month probationary period.

During your probationary period, the office manager will confer with you concerning your job performance. At the conclusion of this period a mutual decision will determine whether or not your employment should be continued.

E. Paid Sick Leave

(_____), Inc. provides six (6) days of paid sick leave per year. Absence due to personal illness for any portion of your scheduled hours will be charged against sick leave on an hour-for-hour basis in quarter-hour increments.

Full-time employees begin earning sick leave from the date of employment at the rate of 1/2 day (4 hours) for each calendar month worked.

You become eligible to receive paid sick leave after you have completed three (3) months of full-time employment.

F. Sexual Harassment

Will not be tolerated. Your safety is insured in the company without fear of losing your job by those in management who might want sexual favors. Report such behavior at once.

G. Leave of Absence

While all employees are expected to exhibit commitment through consci-
entious involvement in ongoing activities of this office, certain extended
absences may be unavoidable. You may be granted a leave of absence for a
variety of reasons for your benefit and that of the organization.

Among other reasons, personal leaves may be granted due to the
death of an immediate family member, to include mother, father, or any
children of you or your spouse. A period of up to three (3) days leave is
granted in these circumstances.

Maternity leaves may be granted for a period not to exceed sixty (60)
calendar days. Prior to the birth of a child you may work as long as your
physician gives written approval to do so. Similarly you may return to
work as soon as you have your physician's approval.

You will be offered the opportunity to return to your position whenever possible if you resume work within thirty (30) days.

H. Resignation and Termination

If you intend to resign, you are expected to give the office at least two (2)
weeks notice. When you terminate you will receive equivalent compensation for all accrued and unused vacation days and sick leave.

If you give less than the expected notice, you are not eligible to receive equivalent compensation for unused vacation and/or sick leave or
other reimbursements.

I. Disciplinary Action

You are expected to observe the scheduled work week. Poor attendance
and/or tardiness will result in disciplinary action. Three absences or tar-
dies or a combination thereof in one month or six in three months, will be
noted as a basis for reprimand. Continued abuse will result in dismissal.

Use of alcohol and or improper or illegal use of drugs on company
property or theft from the business will result in termination.

J. Jury Duty

This is an excused absence.

OFFICE POLICIES

The following policies establish the basic guideline for day-to- day office
operations.

A. Office Hours for Employees

The normal work week is from 8:00 a.m. to 12:00 noon and from 1:00 p.m. to 5:p.m. Monday through Friday.

B. Break Periods

A one hour break from 12:00 noon until 1:00 p.m. is scheduled as an unpaid lunch break.

Two fifteen (15) minute breaks from work with pay are provided daily, one in the morning and one in the afternoon.

C. Absence and Tardiness

You are expected to be present and on time for work daily. However, if absence or tardiness is unavoidable, please notify the office manager as early in the work day as possible of the circumstances.

D. Employee Classification

The benefits of employment described in this handbook are available only to full-time employees. Full-time employment is defined as working approximately 40 hours per week on a regular basis.

EMPLOYEE RECORD

For your information, please record on the following form, details concerning your work attendance.

Vacation

Days accrued as of January 1st	____	____
Vacation days taken January, February, March	____	____
Days accrued as of April 1st	____	____
Vacation days taken April, May, June	____	____
Days accrued as of July 1st	____	____
Vacation days taken July, August, September	____	____
Days accrued as of October 1st	____	____
Vacation days taken October, November, December	____	____

Sick Leave

Hours accrued as of January 1st	____	____
Sick hours taken January, February, March	____	____
Hours accrued as of April 1st	____	____

Sick hours taken April, May, June   _____ _____
Hours accrued as of July 1st   _____ _____
Sick hours taken July, August, September   _____ _____
Hour accrued as of October 1st   _____ _____
Sick hours taken October, November, December _____ _____

Absence

Indicate Dates

_____
_____
_____
_____
_____

Tardiness

Indicate hours missed

_____
_____
_____
_____
_____

Disciplinary Action

Indicate details

_____
_____
_____
_____
_____

Date of Annual Review

_____

Chapter 17

DAY-TO-DAY OPERATIONS
Who Does What and When

You have already gotten a good idea of the many tasks necessary to your business success. But there are nitty-gritty duties that don't ever get spelled out unless we sit down and deliberately look at them. This is what this chapter is about. In Chapter Sixteen we looked at the general duties of each of your workers. In this chapter, we stand at the elbow of each worker, guiding them through specific operations as if it were their first day.

CASHIER

Writing up the daily cash deposits

Payments are batched into groups of 40. Two tapes are then run, one with the checks and one with the deposit slips. If they agree, the checks and statements then have separate batch headers attached. The batch number is placed in the book. The statements are then entered into a shipping record or on a computer or into a record-keeping journal.

If any of the payments are NSF checks, resubmit the check for a second time. If you have it come through a second time, call the customer and explain that they need to send a money order or a check from a different checking account. Don't mail the product until the check has cleared the bank.

In making cash deposits use a batch number system to keep from getting confused. Let's use two companies, Company Limited and Tribute Incorporated, for example. Use three different identifying numbers for each company as well as their company names.

BATCH NUMBERING SYSTEM

Company	First Digit	
Company Limited	6	Cash
	7	American Express
	9	Visa-Master Card
Tribute Inc.	1	Cash
	2	American Express
	4	Visa-Master Card
Etc.	3	Cash
	5	American Express
	8	Visa-Master Card

The next digit of the batch number is the date of the Julian year for all companies. (Julian meaning the actual day of the year, such as Jan. 1, 1987 is 001; May 3 is 123.). The last two digits signify the current batch being worked on for the day. The cashier might do 6 deposit sheets in one day. The first one would end in 01, then 02 and so on. The batch number would be 9 123 06. Interpreted: the company deposit was Company Limited, payment was by Visa-Mastercard, it was May 3, and there were 6 deposits made that day.

THE DEPOSIT RECORD MUST BE FILLED IN EACH DAY

The example numbers that represent cash, 6 for Company Limited, 1 for Tribute Inc. and 3 for another company or division would be handled by the cash and refund cashier. Then the credit card cashier would use in Company Limited 7 for American Express, 9 for Visa-Mastercard; Tribute Inc. would use 2 for American Express, 4 for Visa-Mastercard and the third company or division would use 5 for American Express and 8 for Visa-Mastercard etc. After the deposits are done the information must be placed in the record-keeping device. The following information has to be entered into the computer or record-keeping device and perhaps on your shipping record as well:

1. The actual amount of money received
2. Cancellation with order: (a regular payment for one shipment but the customer doesn't want any additional product)
3. Straight cancel
4. Changes with payment (like a new address)

5. Pre-payments (money up front from the customer)
6. Open billing (meaning the customer has credit from your company and won't be charged until they receive the product)
7. Any kind of changes (such as new gift donors, recipient or removal of recipient or donor)
8. Duplicate payments. If duplicated, pull their file and follow duplication procedure: If a check, send a letter and return the check. If payment is made by credit card, destroy credit card authorization, give credit for the next product shipment, or ask if they would like to buy another shipment and treat the payment as a pre-payment.

After the money transactions have been put into your record- keeping device, divide the money into two piles: cash payments and credit card payments. It is a good idea to keep a notebook with this information put into it each day. That way you have a running account of your cash flow and you can see it in an instant. You will immediately know how much cash you have on hand and how much money you are due (called a receivable).

Below I have provided you with a "Record of Deposit" sheet. When you have put your batches of 40 together then it is handy to have the record of deposit sheet. This way you can add up the daily batches. This is handy in that at the end of the month it is easy to check your bank statement against them.

RECORD OF DEPOSITS   Example
Tribute Inc.   **Date**
                                Sheet No. 05

Batch No.   Dollar Amount
4 124 03   300.00
2 124 04   1000.00
1 124 05   57.00

                                   1357.00
                      Total Amount for the day

At the end of the month, the cashier will need to make out the statements to those who have open-billing. This can be done by hand or generated by a computer program. Then the statements will be given to the manager who will see that they are mailed. The statements will be in a collection series. For each number in the series—let's say 6—there will be the corresponding letter that will be sent along with it. The sample letters follow.

#1

THANK YOU .

It was a real pleasure to send you the . package recently. I know
it adds or added a great deal of pleasure to your family life.

I always try to serve you the way one good neighbor serves
another. Your continued friendship and goodwill are most
important to me and to our company.

When you send payment for your last (name of item), please
return the enclosed statement with your check. It identifies
your account so I can quickly mark it "Paid In Full" just as
soon as payment is received. Use the handy reply envelope I've
included.

Your prompt attention is most appreciated.

Sincerely yours,

Name of President

#2

Dear Plate Collector: (or Van Owner/Homemaker/Etc.)

It was a bit of a surprise, in view of your excellent credit
standing, to see your account come past due. Possibly there's a
mistake on my part. I try to be as accurate as possible in
billing, but sometimes an error will creep in.

I have enjoyed sending you these beautiful (name of product) so
do let me know if there is something wrong. If not, please send
your check and I'll mark your account "Paid In Full".

Thank you so much,

Name of President

If you have not received payment by the second letter use the

Telephone Script

Mr. and/or Mrs. _____

This is _____ **(Name)** with the **(Name of Company)** I'm
calling in regard to your **name of product.** Did you receive your
shipment? **Wait** (if answer is no, tell them you'll send a tracer,
Note here: Products that are sent by the post office are very
hard to trace so be careful. . . .If answer is yes, continue as
follows). We are now ending the order processing for this
shipment and our records indicate that payment for your
shipment has not been received.

(Wait for comment). I have written you several times, but have
as yet not received your payment. I would be glad to take
payment by your Visa or Mastercard or your American Express
number now. **(Wait)** If you prefer, mail your check today. Can we
count on you to send the payment today? We should receive it
about _____ . We appreciate your taking
care of this bill immediately. The **(name of company)** wants you
to continue to enjoy our product. If we can be of further
assistance please let us know.

#3

Dear Customer,

Twelve weeks ago you received the latest shipment of our
(product). The invoice was on the top of the box. Since that time
I have not received payment.

I'm sure you would like to settle this situation. Enclosed is the
statement of your account. Just send payment, and we'll be all
square and even.

[If you add products to the line, this statement could be
inserted: If, for some reason, you do not care to keep this latest
(product) please return it. Just place (the product) in its
shipping container and put it with our regular outgoing mail.
Just as soon as I receive the product, I'll clear your account and
you'll owe nothing.]

So, please let me hear from you one way or the other. Send payment, or return the product. Please let me hear back from you today.

Sincerely,

Name of President

#4

Dear Mr. _____:
(Note: at this point, begin calling the customer by name in the salutation)

This morning your statement was put on my desk again still marked **UNPAID.** To protect your credit standing, I strongly urge you to send your payment today.

You cannot expect us to wait any longer. I urge you to send payment now. Your account must be cleared today.

Sincerely,

Name of President

#5

Dear Mr. _____

Your account has been sitting on my desk for two months waiting for your payment.

I'm sure neither one of us wants this to go on indefinitely. Pay your invoice today. Just as soon as I receive the payment, the account will be cleared.

Sincerely,

Name of President

#6

Dear Mr. _____

Four months ago your (name of product) was shipped to you.
The bill was on the top of the box. Since then I have written you
six times, but your account remains unpaid. We cannot let this
account go unpaid indefinitely.

Your credit standing in your community is important. Protect it.
Send payment today.

Yours truly,

Name of President

#7

Dear Mr. _____

This is the seventh letter I have written asking for your
payment. You have said nothing, but I can wait no longer.

Unless I receive your payment within the next ten (10) days, I
will have no choice. Your account will be turned over to the law
firm of (SO AND SO) for collection.

Surely you do not want legal problems. Surely you do not want
your credit rating damaged. Send payment today.

Sincerely,

Name of President

AND I promise you if you say you're going to do it, DO IT. It is against the law not to. Have some sort of collection agency ready so that they can follow through. A collection agency usually charges 25% the first 6 months and after that, 50%. At least you get part of your money back. You will be surprised how many people will respond . . . Don't keep them as future customers.

CREDIT CARD CASHIER

For American Express

1. Type (or write) charge slips. Be sure to type numbers in groups. "On file" is typed on approval code line. Card member's full name and account number is shown in the card member space. Type name of product and product number out beside the name or account number space. Show amount of charge in the total space on the bottom line.
2. Run tapes for each batch. Tape total should agree with proof list total. Write order batch number on tape, cross out any charges pulled and correct the total.
3. Keep separated by batches. Run tapes on each batch.
4. Run on imprinter.
5. Separate soft and hard copies.
6. Run tapes on hard copies. Tapes should agree.
7. Make a batch summary for each bundle, using batch header card on imprinter. Mark the batch numbers submitted under this header on the copy you keep.
8. Post each batch summary on the summary sheet for your records.
9. Mail hard copies to American Express.

Note: Be sure to use the correct machine imprinter. The American Express imprinter is the one that has a date. Make sure the date is changed before running cards.

For Visa-Mastercard

1. Type (or write) charge slips. Both these charge slips must show an expiration date typed immediately below the card account number. The customer's full name and address must be typed two spaces below. Date of charge is typed in space provided. Show the name of the product and pack number in the descrip-

tion space. Type the amount of charge in the "total" line at bottom of slip. Type "mail order" in the signature space.

2. Charges over $50 dollars must have authorization codes before being submitted. All others do not need authorization codes, as the bank will get them for you.

3. Follow steps 2 through 8 as for American Express.

9. Make deposit slips using one original and two carbons. Show gross amount of deposit less % you have been allotted (discount-net deposit).

10. When credits are being submitted with charges, show gross amount of charges, gross amount of credits, net sales, less % discount-net deposit for Visa and Mastercard. Send one continuous tape to the bank showing sub-total and credit subtracted, thus showing the total of tape as the gross amount.

11. Two copies of batch header and two copies of deposit slip go to the bank. Batch header must show checking account number.

12. Give hard copies with deposit slips to whoever takes the deposit to the bank. Batch header must show checking account number.

13. Post on summary sheet and make a photocopy for the office.

Credit Memos

Follow same procedure as for typing charges. Submit with charges whenever possible, but in any case, be sure to submit any needed credits each week. (1) Send pink copy to be filed with customer's file. (2) Keep remaining copies with tape. (3) Send hard copy to credit card company. Send customer a photocopy of credit slip and write a letter advising him credit has been issued. You might also want to mention to him that sometimes it takes two cycles from the credit card company for that credit to show up, so be patient.

Invalid accounts; declines, non-clearable checks, etc.

When declines and invalid account charges are returned to you, these are called charge backs. Follow through with these steps.

1. Pull order card and certify number and expiration date. If error is found in either, resubmit with correct number or date. If an error is found, contact customer to verify the number. In spaces below, date charge is typed in space provided. Show name and number to contact, assume merchandise has been delivered and bill direct.

2. To bill direct, send letter asking for payment to replace declined credit card change. Put customer's file in credit card folder and make a cross reference sheet to go in regular file. Make notation

in shipping journal to check credit card folder before processing new order for this customer.

3. When check is received to replace declined credit card, release label—if it has been held. (1.) Record payment on log sheet in credit card folder. (2.) Mark payment on copy of last letter sent to customer. (3.) Answer any questions or complaint the customer has.

4. If a corrected card number or expiration date is received on a direct billing, resubmit charge.

Resubmitting charges

1. Type new charge slips and attach one copy to debit slip from bank.

2. Mark batch number used to resubmit charges on face of debit slip and file in credit card file.

Follow up on direct billings

1. On the first and third Wednesdays of each month, check credit card folders and send reminders to any persons who have been previously contacted and have not responded.

2. After the third attempt, if there is still no response, make a DSP/N (Bad Debt Code) and send to the computer or make an entry in your financial journal. Post DSP or bad debt in shipping journal and advise the customer that if the account is not paid in ten days it will be turned over for collection. Any future orders from this customer must be accompanied by cash before order can be processed.

3. On pre-arranged credit card customers, the computer will send a print-out or credit cards and their numbers so that charges can be submitted at shipping time. If you do not have this program, have the charges typed up ahead of time so that they will be ready to submit at the time of shipment.

At the end of the month the credit card cashier checks the credit deposits against the bank statement to make sure they are correct. If possible talk to your banker and ask him/her to resubmit the charges twice before a charge back is issued. The reason for this is that often a payment a customer sends to Visa- Mastercard hasn't been credited yet so it bounces, but if the charges are resubmitted, they will go through. Charge backs cost money so find out from your bank how much that service costs ahead of time. Anything you can do to cut this cost is good.

EXAMPLE OF WHAT A VISA BATCH HEADER LOOKS LIKE

```
300772        300772          VISA BATCH HEADER
```

	AMOUNT
0227 BAC GALLERY EDITIONS LIMITED TOTAL SALES DRAFTS	156 00
LESS CREDIT DRAFTS	272 00
NET SALES	116 00 -
LESS _3_ % DISCOUNT	3 48
NET DEPOSIT	(112 52-)

HC11817780
EA0227300772
GALLERY EDITION
LIMITED
MCALLEN, TEXAS

Completion of this form and enclosure herein of the sales drafts shall constitute endorsement and delivery of such sales drafts pursuant to the BankAmericard member agreement entered into between Bank of the Southwest N.A. and the depositor. Deposit is accepted subject to verification and correction.

X _____ CHECKING ACCOUNT NUMBER

DATE March 25 ____ 19__

Example of Batch Header When Credits Equal More Than Charges

The net deposit amount will always be shown as a minus amount enclosed in brackets, whenever the amount of credits is greater than the charges, or whenever credits are being submitted without charges.

DIRECT MARKETING TYPIST

Filing

Payments, correspondence, complaints, and compliments—all mail that comes into the office is filed, including new orders with their key numbers, and customer phone problems that have been written down in the office.

a. Have several wire baskets in the office. Put the correspondence into them first. Divide baskets into different groups, clean up, check addresses, then use the divider board to put all correspondence into zip codes. This is called the zip- code-last-name procedure. See Chapter Fourteen for an explanation of this filing system. Then stack the correspondence in that order. Place a note on top of the pile stating it is in order. When the filing is ready for the file cabinets, or whatever storage you have prepared to hold your documents, you look under the zip code number to see if any correspondence matches any existing file. New filing should be placed toward the front of that zip, in alphabetical order.

b. Any name or zip changes need to be cross-referenced where old file was; then place complete file under the new name or address.

Calling Procedure For Collections

1. Collection letter #3 requires a personal telephone call to the customer.
2. First look up the area code of the customer.
3. If the customer is not listed (NL) or the listing is not published (NP) send the 3rd statement immediately.
4. Begin calling.
5. After the customer has been reached, send the statement. The marketing typist types up the collection letters for the cashier to enclose with the statement. The collection letters are provided with the cashier work sheets.

One of the most important duties of the marketing typist is to record the key numbers as they come into the officer on a separate sheet. Key numbers, called "list response" are discussed in Chapter Four. It will be the direct marketing manager's duty then to analyze them for future selection. She will also keep count on a calendar of how many come in each day so that the marketing manager can forecast how many sales will be made from the mailing. She also keeps up with the white mail. White mail is what the correspondence from a customer is called. These letters should be answered within a few days. When someone has taken the time to sit down and write to the company it is important. You will have a lot of variety but if you make up several types of letters (form letters), that will help.

Here's a sample:

```
Dear Mrs. (type in the name to make it more personal)

Thank you for your order. You can rest assured that your gift
will be given our total care and attention. If we can help you in
any further way please let us know.

                                        Your friend,


                                        Name of President
```

As your correspondence begins to come in, the types of letters will become easy to identify. At that time it would be a good idea for you or the marketing manager to draft some letters to fit the needs.

The other responsibility of the marketing typist is to type the drafts.

The most important thing she does is open the mail. It is very important that the mail be dated right away. And the mail is sorted into payments, white mail, orders, etc.

She will type acknowledgements. If the product will not be shipped within 30 days after the literature states then the 30- day rule takes over. The secretary will write these people giving them a chance to cancel or wait for the product.

The marketing secretary also checks the new orders against a print-out sheet (if by computer—called a shipping record) or manually if set up that way. The proof list is checked against the original order. If it is correct, the order is filled with the above procedure. There should be two print-out sheets, one in alphabetical order and the other one by zip sequence.

The labels accompany the proof list (how to check).

Layout the shipping record-orders and labels, then separate the batches. Check for amount due, price, product number, address, route number, and the account number.

Procedure for donor/recipient—pull the donor's label, then get a blank label and type the recipient's address, pack number, routing, and the donor's name and address showing it is a gift. The donor's label is then used for billing with the recipient's name and address on it to acknowledge who the product was shipped to.

Check to see that everyone has a label. If not,

1. Type a label for that order, and write on the shipping record the information needed.
2. Then make a list of these people so that the information can be put either in a computer or into your record keeping journal. Create a record for this customer and credit their account if payment has already been made.

GENERAL TYPIST RESPONSIBILITIES

He or she will handle all the overflow that the marketing typist can't do.

The general typist will do all the record-keeping associated with the business not customer-related, in other words, office business such as gas, electricity, and insurance bills. This type of filing is well done in alphabetical order. No one has ever figured out anything much better than your basic manila folder, with the tab clearly marked for what's inside. Thus, you'll have a drawer in the file cabinet, or an expandable cardboard file, or a cardboard box in which a folder marked "Electricity" will be followed by one called "Insurance" followed with one called "Loans," and so forth.

Most people put the latest thing in the front of the folder. If you have information that goes together, paper-clip it rather than staple. However you organize, try to be consistent, making a few notes to yourself at first if you think you'll forget from one filing to the next how you've organized.

The other way to file is chronologically, by day, month, year—whatever fits what information you're wanting to save. In this category go such items as computer hard-copy print-out books of your records, your daily deposit sheets, and record books from freight carriers etc. This is where the shelf space comes in. Be sure you have plenty of space for saving.

The general typist files the forms for United Parcel if and when it is used. She also does all functions required for the United States Post Office as well. These functions will consist of filing all forms from both United Parcel Service and the United States Postal Service.

It is very difficult to trace anything from the United States Postal Service. However, if there is art work or important papers, they should be registered. The Postal Service also provides express mail service.

Federal Express is another way to go. The typist simply calls them and they will pick up right away.

If a customer or supplier wants something sent back by way of the post office, the general typist sends a "receipt return requested" tag to them. They place the tag on the item and mail it. If you have shipped perishable goods and they are being returned, the post office will call you to come look at the returned goods. However,they will then be destroyed. In this case nothing will be used again. The obvious reason for this is the possibility of food poisoning and/or tampering. If you are shipping a product such as grapefruit spoons and the customer doesn't want them and you have shipped by the post office you can send a "receipt return requested" tag to the customer so they may return the product.

If you have mailed these spoons by UPS the return procedure is as follows:

    a. The product is opened. A return product sheet is filled in (the sheet is green and must contain all necessary information).

    b. The customer's file is pulled. The reason for the return is noted. If the customer does not say why he no longer wants the product, a telephone call is made or a letter is written immediately to find out.

The general typist logs into the log book the date, last name, zip code, and product number of the returned product. It should be noted whether the product is cancelled, undeliverable or damaged.

Record all information in correct shipping log. If it's a cancel, mark it and place in a separate box. If it's a cancel and refund do the same, put original file in REFUND basket to be refunded. If it was returned for credit, give original file to cashier so she can issue a CREDIT.

UNDELIVERABLE:

The customer is contacted and the information is noted in the shipping record and the original file is filed until further notice from the customer. Product is held until further notice.

IF AN ITEM IS TO BE REPLACED:

The customer is notified as to when to expect the replacement, immediately or in several weeks.

DAMAGED PRODUCT SENT BY UPS:

   a. File a claim.
   b. Provide a copy of the shipping record.
   c. Make three copies of the UPS pick-up record. (a pink and blue billing sheet). Send a copy to your regional UPS office, file a copy and keep one at your desk. The procedure takes about 60 days before payment.

LOST OR OTHER:

   a. First contact the customer. After the tracer has been returned, look to see who signed it. If it is the same signature, write a letter to the customer with a copy of the tracer that shows his signature and date of delivery. If he denies it, then place a claim of denial. Payment follows.
   b. If it is a different signature on the tracer, try to contact the customer to ask if he knows the person who signed. If not, the same product will be shipped to them.

CALL TAGS:

The bright yellow call tag is used when a customer says they won't send the product back unless your business calls for it. Make 3 copies—file one, send original, and keep one at the desk. The problem should be noted on each copy.

BROKEN PRODUCT:

If the product is broken, and was sent by parcel post, the procedure is to have the product returned and your company will replace the product.

However, UPS is contacted to pick the article up. Each UPS product is given an LDI number (a claim number that identifies the claim). UPS will repay your company for the damage.

TRACERS:

a. Tracers are white forms used for UPS only. These are filled out and sent to UPS. Always use the shipper number (example 762-362). This number will be given the business when it begins using UPS.

b. United States Postal System tracers. Product can now be traced through Post Office only to determine whether or not the customer received product. To trace we need name and address of customer, product price and its pack number. Tracers go to your hometown post office.

MONTHLY SHIPPING ANALYSIS:

This is a summary sheet with the date of the week, returned product, cancels, and how many packages of product have been shipped for that month. Also, shipping summary sheets should be made after large shipments of product that went open-billing or pre-paid for monthly receivables. These sheets are checked against the tally sheets for correct numbers shipped.

POSTAGE BILLING

The general typist checks to see how much postage is used each month. And if someone is doing your drop-shipping for you, check closely to see if it is correct. Drop-shipping means someone is actually physically shipping your product for you.

TELEPHONE AND TELEPHONE MARKETING

1. When a customer wants to order over the phone I have found the following procedure very helpful. Talk to your customer. Take as much time as you need to. Don't hurry because the customer will know and she will feel she's not important and that's the most important part of the telephone marketer—making the customer feel important. Next, use the form shown attached to record information.

Always end the conversation with a smile in your voice and reassure your customer you are taking good care of them.

2. Each morning take the names of the people who have called on

the answering machine and dial them right away. The one time that a person calls is perhaps the only time he or she will try. Don't let them get away. Keep trying until you reach them.

3. From time to time it is a good idea to call your customers—with a new offer—especially if you have the manpower. CUSTOMER SERVICE IS THE KEY. THAT'S WHAT YOUR BUSINESS IS —DO IT!

BOOKKEEPER

1. One of the chief duties of the bookkeeper or the function of book-keeping is the monthly report. I know it seems like a lot of extra work but it's amazing how you can keep up with your business this way. Below is a good way to do it. You will have lots of ways in which to do record keeping: this is a quick overview of the entire business.

PAGE ONE

NAME (Tribute Inc.)
Enclosed are the records of deposits, the accounts receivable, and the inventory. Example Product and boxes in stock Nov.

Pack A (Product)	How much left in the warehouse
Pack AB (Product)	Same
Pack A Boxes	345
Pack AB Boxes	1087
Total	_____

PAGE TWO

PACK A PRODUCT SHIPMENTS SHIPPED OPEN BILLING
NONE

PACK AB PRODUCT SHIPMENTS SHIPPED OPEN BILLING
1

RESHIPMENT OF
PACK A
PACK AB

PACKAGES OF PRODUCT SHIPPED NON OPEN BILLING
PACK A   5005
PACK AB 2500

PAGE THREE

Tribute Inc. Accounts Receivable

PACK A	Balance last month	3310.00
	Payments	
	Cancels	
	New Balance	_____
PACK AB	Balance last month	
	Payments	
	Cancels	
	New Balance	_____

and so on

GRAND TOTAL _____

PAGE FOUR

TRIBUTE INC. COLLECTIONS
PACK A BALANCE   5100.00
PACK AB BALANCE   0.00

PAGE FIVE

PACK A REFUNDS
PACK AB REFUNDS

PAGE SIX

TRIBUTE INC.
RECORD OF DEPOSITS

DATE
EXAMPLE   SHEET NUMBER

(number of checks)	dollar (amt)	description of product	batch no.
1	$24.98	Pack A	B#609141
14	amt	same	B#609103

TOTAL _____

There should be deposit slips for each day of the month. You will have 28 to 31 record-of-deposit sheets in your report.

PAGE SEVEN

THE RECORD OF ALL YOUR CHARGES AND CREDITS
    VISA AND MASTERCARD
    DATE BATCH# PACK CHARGES CREDITS DEPOSITS

    AMERICAN EXPRESS
    DATE BATCH# PACK GROSS CHARGES CREDITS

PAGE EIGHT

SPREAD SHEET SHOWING EACH PACK SHIPPED THE MONTH OF THE YEAR PACK A   PACK AB   TOTALED SHIPPED   TOTAL PAYMENTS AND CANCELS ACCOUNTS RECEIVABLES TO DATE   CHARGE OFF'S BAD DEBT

The bookkeeper will make out all the payroll except where you can find a service to do it for you instead.

The bookkeeper keeps track of workdays, sick days, etc.

SHIPPING CLERK

Shipping
    a   first labels are run through the postage meter by UPS and Parcel Post according to zones. Then labels go back to the manager to be put onto proper boxes for shipment.
    b. a tally sheet is kept as to when the shipment leaves, the price of the pack, and the number shipped. This is given to the general typist at the end of each day.
    c. an inventory is checked at the end of the month of all product, packaging, business paper (such as envelopes, stationery, etc.).
    d. the shipping clerk also inserts any invoices or statements that may need to go out of the office. They can be inserted by hand or by an inserting machine. Once they are inserted they are given to the office manager for processing, then mailing.

ORDER LOG

BATCH NUMBER	FIRST ORDER NUMBER	LAST ORDER NUMBER	PACK NUMBER	DATE	C A S H	A M E X	M C	TOTAL TO DATE

Gallery Edition Ltd.
COMPANY

Inventory SHEET
ISSUE

DATE

ARS		MIM		MRG	
Cathedral	1	Michelangelo	180	Lavender Lace	620
First Edition	12	Mrs. John Douglass	9	Cuddles	148
Charisma	99	Don Antonio Noriega	3	Rise-n-Shine	2
Paradise	98	Lovely Reader	78	Peaches-n-Cream	33
Sundowner	28	Gingerbread Santa	8	Pacesetter	20
Friendship	96	M+C 80'	60	Total MRG	823
Love	97	M+C 81'	164		
Honor	97	M+C 82'	481	DBD	
Cherish	97	M+C 83'	752	First Slippers	584
Bing Crosby	94	Total MIM	1,735		Ware-H 1,296
White Lightnin'	100	Superheroes		At the Barre	796
Marina	98	Superman	4	The Recital	515
Shreveport	347	Total Super-H	4	Pirouette	230
French Lace	263			Swan Lake	241
Brandy	138			Total DBD	3,662
Mon Cheri	136				
Sweet Surrender	163				
Sun Flare	131				
Impatient	47				
Olympiad	5				
Total ARS	2,147			Grand Total	8,371
			271		

TELEPHONE
INQUIRY

PERSON TAKING CALL   DATE

NAME OF PERSON & FIRM

MAILING ADDRESS   STREET   BOX NO.

CITY   STATE   ZIP CODE

ACCOUNT NO.   TELEPHONE NUMBER   AM. EXPRESS CREDIT CARD NO.

☐ COMPLAINT   ☐ INQUIRY

REMARKS:

Chapter 18

INSURANCE
Safe-proofing your Efforts

Insurance...Insurance...Insurance.
This may not be the most exciting chapter of the book, but it's the last chapter and it's short. No! Don't put it down: you really need to read the chapter. Unfortunately to be in business today you must have insurance. And several different types.

The purpose of insurance is to protect you and to protect your product, office and equipment. You will only need as much insurance as you feel you can gamble on. You must decide how much risk you can take or how much risk you want to take.

Insurance can be costly. On the other hand if you aren't properly insured it will cost you an arm and a leg if you have any property loss. Shop around for competitive rates.

In your office, be it in your home, or away from your home, you will need:

1. fire insurance
2. theft insurance including office equipment
3. security insurance
4. product insurance
5. car insurance
6. employee insurance

Fire insurance and theft insurance pretty well explain themselves. Security insurance includes a good alarm system against break-ins and a good fire–proof safe to protect your records. The institution ("They") studies have proven thieves oftentimes are warded off just knowing a place of business has an alarm system. The alarm people say it deters around 80% of thieves. What better insurance can there be as well as for your peace of mind?

Insurance

One of the most important insurance policies you will need to carry will be to protect your product. You will need product insurance while the product is:

1. being warehoused
2. in transit from the manufacturer
3. being sent to your customer
4. in the hands of your customer

Some insurance brokers can combine several types of protection into one so try to accomplish just that.

Some insurance companies will take inventory at the beginning of each month and only charge you insurance against what you have in the warehouse. This type of insurance is really important especially if you're into something fragile such as glass and china. With this type of insurance you only pay for what you have warehoused at the time. Can't you just see a whole shelf of china falling to the ground and breaking into a million pieces. Won't they ever stop breaking? It seems like an eternity and there's nothing you can do about it. Here goes your year's preparation of your product down the drain and you need to sell and be shipping the product now. What will you do? You may lose the current business sales, but aren't you glad you have warehousing insurance? At least you'll have the money to replace the product and hopefully with a good letter to your customer explaining your dilemma he/she will wait until the item can be remanufactured.

Intransit insurance for a product that's on its way to you is equally important. A fire in the truck or traffic accident and you have no product. Some companies insure their trucks for that reason so perhaps the insurance coverage is already in place. Check on this one before you double-insure.

The other intransit insurance is on the product being shipped to your customer. Being in a family business for over 35 years, we had a time or two when a truck turned over. One instance I recall was a truck loaded with products that came up to a bridge and jack-knifed. The truck turned over and caught fire and the shipment was totally destroyed. The driver just escaped death. Not only did the insurance pay for the damage, saving the company large losses, but because of the good computer system, within two hours every box of product and who it was to be delivered to had been identified so that the customers could be notified. Immediately new boxes of fruit were being placed upon a new truck.

Consumer liability insurance protects you in case a customer becomes ill or injured from using your product. For example, if they have eaten off your product (such as a plate) and claimed to have been poisoned by the finish or gotten cut from a knife you sold them, they may decide to sue you. A good case in point is the recent scare of a china company from Italy. The finish on the china was inferior and the lead testing didn't meet industry standards. The plate manufacturer's policy was a major disaster and the china has had to be recalled. Can you imagine the impact on that poor company's business?

The china for all the companies I represented had to meet these standards so I am well aware of the time and expense it takes to meet them. Some companies try to cut corners, as this Italian company did. You must decide if you want to insure yourself against this type of situation. If you don't want to go through standard testing, then let your customers know up front. In any case, take out insurance.

Car insurance goes without saying. If you or anyone working for you gets into an accident, the medical costs involved let alone any liable injury or death could destroy you. Employee insurance includes:

1. Health insurance
2. Workmen's Compensation
3. Unemployment Insurance
4. Personal Liability Insurance

In the state of Texas, and probably in your home state, these four types of insurance are set up to help the employer and the employee. If you or an employee is hurt or injured on the job, workmen's compensation can be a life saver.

If you have your office in your home, you can have a rider put on your personal homeowner's liability policy to include your business. This way a person coming to your home office to work who might fall and break a leg will be covered. They can sue the business but not you personally.

In some states when you pay your quarterly employment taxes and your employee's social security tax, some money may go to pay for unemployment insurance. So if you or your employees are suddenly out of work, you can draw unemployment pay.

Well, here you have it. I'm sure there are other insurance possibilities that are specialized just for your type of business, but these are four that I recommend to you for your safekeeping while you are in business.

I know you are going to be happy and successful. If, after reading this book you find you want additional help, look in the back for more background on the Direct Marketing Association. They are great folks and can help you in any number of areas.

I'm looking forward to getting your advertising in the mail. I know I just can't live without your product.

IN CLOSING

This book is unique in the direct marketing field. Every other how-to mail order book is so advanced that the reader must know the basics of direct mail marketing *before* using the book. My book is dedicated to you, the rank beginner—the person with not much more than a gambler's spirit and a burning desire to sell something through the mail. It is a basic 1-2-3, do-able, Direct Marketing Book.

Remember I began with front end analyzing—armchair projection, considerations, worksheets, upfront sobering and exhilarating facts and figures. "Part II: Doing Business" guides you through your first-year operation—a service for which consultants of new firms easily receive thousands of dollars. The third section, "Money Money Money Everywhere?" guides you the beginner on how to handle business finances. Part IV, "Back End Analyzing," ensures the business health and success. Lastly, "Part V: Fine-Tuning Your Operation" ensures that the entrepreneur (you) will be a long-range success through wise management of office, personnel, data and shipping.

Keep this book close to you at all times as a quick and easy reference. Satisfaction Guaranteed!

DMA
Direct Marketing Association

Some sixty years ago it started as an association of mail order people, people who sold and delivered their products by mail. There were the general merchandise firms with catalogs, and small specialty firms selling everything from lobsters to newsletters by mail.

During the 1930's this industry grew. There were mail order suppliers: envelope manufacturers, copywriters, mailing houses. These firms served the mail order marketers.

Since these people and firms had a common interest in selling by direct mail, they all had a strong interest in the U.S. mail, how it operated and what it charged for its services. A common industry voice was needed and the Direct Mail Marketing Association was formed.

Over the years the organization has grown and changed. Today it's not just mail order marketing, but direct marketing. There's phone marketing, television marketing, consumer marketing and business-to-business marketing—truly direct marketing. Most major advertising agencies now have a direct marketing division. Most major department stores print beautiful catalogs and now sell their products nationally by mail.

Still the backbone of the Direct Marketing Association is Mail Order. For every major account member there are fifty small "mail order" members. Each year sees a number of new start-up members . . . and each year sees a few fall by the wayside.

To pinpoint its now far reaching services the Direct Marketing Association has developed special interest groups. There is a group discussing catalog production, or research and evaluation, or business to business sales, or telemarketing, or selling through television, magazines, newspapers and package inserts.

The Association's Basic Institutes are held across the nation each year. These $3^1/2$ days of intensive classroom, problem-solving sessions are indepth courses for beginners.

For the beginner doing "Business On The Kitchen Table" these institutes sharpen skills and knowledge of this method of marketing.

The Association Direct Mail Marketing Manuals, which every member receives, are designed to keep you up to date on the latest techniques. There are over 120 reports divided into 15 different categories. Each brief report is written by an expert in the field. Whether you are interested in small direct mail business management overviews, printing laser beam personal letters, or selecting new products for your next mailing, you'll find good words of guidance from the people who know how.

Naturally, you'll learn that all good mail order businesses must have a good offer . . . and here's the Direct Marketing Association's offer. Just call 212-689-4977 and ask for new member services. You'll receive a whole bundle of how-to-do-it-right information, and it's FREE.

Oh yes, always remember to include the name and address. In this case:

Direct Marketing Association
6 East 43rd Street
New York, New York 10017

INDEX
Direct Mail Marketing Terms

Mail Order On The Kitchen Table
Startup And Navigational HELP

Startup

　　To start the stack, start up HyperCard and insert the program disk into any drive and double-click on the stack titled "Mail Order". This will take you to the title page of the stack. From there, click on the Open Book button in the upper right hand corner of the screen and you will go to the "Table Of Contents". This is the card you will revolve around as you go from program to program. To go to one of the programs, just click on the title of your choice.

Navigation

　　This stack is set up in book form. You will be looking at a portion of a page as you do the worksheets. When a worksheet is too large to fit on one screen, there will be navigational arrows in the corner of the page you are looking at. These arrows will take you to the other sections of the worksheet. When you have finished a worksheet, click on the "Table Of Contents" button to go there and make your next choice.

MACINTOSH

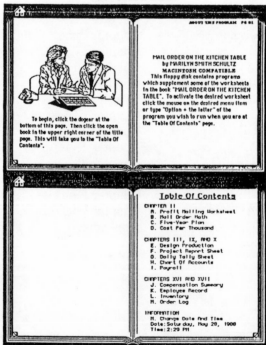

Mail Order on the Kitchen Table
By
Marilyn Smith Schultz

General Instructions for Using the Program Disk.

1. Make a working copy of the program disk and store the original.

2. Be sure that you have a CONFIG.SYS file with FILES = 20 and BUFFERS = 20 on your DOS boot disk. You can check this on a hard disk system by typing at the C: prompt TYPE CONFIG.SYS. If the file is present it will be typed on the screen. On a two floppy system type the same thing TYPE CONFIG.SYS at the A: prompt. You need FILES = 20 and BUFFERS = 20 as a minimum. Anything larger is O.K. If you do not have this file, you can copy the one from the program disk or check your DOS Manual on how to create one. You must reboot your system with this file on your boot disk.

3. For HARD DISK SYSTEMS
    a. Insert the working copy of the program disk in drive A and change from the C drive to the A drive. Then at the A prompt (A: >) type NEWDRIVE C:
    b. Type COPY GO.EXE C:
    c. Change to the C: drive
    d. Type GO to run the program
    e. Select option O and change the default drive to C: (working disk still in A:)
    f. Repeat step e (This must be done to record the drive change on C:)
    g. Make your next selection.
    h. Program will now run from the C: drive without any other modifications.

4. For TWO FLOPPY DRIVE SYSTEMS
    a. Insert the working copy in drive A and a blank formatted disk in drive B.
    b. At the A prompt type NEWDRIVE B:. This will copy the necessary database files to your disk in drive B.
    c. Type GO to run the program
    d. The default drive has been set to drive A:, and you will need to select option O and change the drive to B when you choose options G, I, L, or M. If you forget to do this, the program will tell you that it can not find certain files. When this happens select O and change the drive to B.

Hard disk systems

C>TYPE CONFIG.SYS	
FILES=20	CONFIG.SYS file present and O.K.
BUFFERS=20	
C>A:	Change from C drive to A drive
A>NEWDRIVE C:	Copies DBF files from A to C
A>COPY GO. EXE C:	Copies main program GO from A to C
A>C:	Change from A drive to C drive
C>GO	Executes the program
Menu on screen	Select option O and change drive to C
	Select option O and change drive to C

Program is now installed on hard disk and needs no other modifications.

TWO FLOPPY SYSTEM

Boot system and with boot disk in drive A do the following:

A>TYPE CONFIG.SYS	
FILES=20	CONFIG.SYS file is O.K.
BUFFERS=20	

Remove boot disk and insert working copy of program disk.

Insert blank formatted disk in drive B:

A>NEWDRIVE B:	Copies DBF files to drive B
A>GO	Executes program
Menu on screen.	Select O and change drive to B

Program now ready to work with working copy in drive A and data disk in drive B.

A NEW approach to Direct Mail Marketing. Just punch "Go" and your floppy disk will print out and calculate the above menu data.

IBM COMPATIBLE

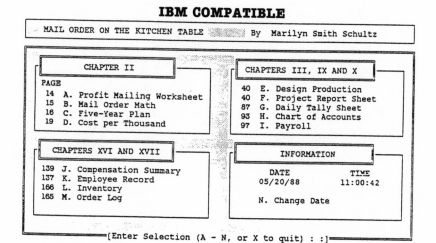

MAIL ORDER ON THE KITCHEN TABLE   By Marilyn Smith Schultz

```
┌─ CHAPTER II ─────────────────┐   ┌─ CHAPTERS III, IX AND X ─────┐
│ PAGE                         │   │   40  E. Design Production    │
│   14  A. Profit Mailing Worksheet │ 40  F. Project Report Sheet  │
│   15  B. Mail Order Math     │   │   87  G. Daily Tally Sheet    │
│   16  C. Five-Year Plan      │   │   93  H. Chart of Accounts    │
│   19  D. Cost per Thousand   │   │   97  I. Payroll              │
└──────────────────────────────┘   └──────────────────────────────┘

┌─ CHAPTERS XVI AND XVII ──────┐   ┌─ INFORMATION ────────────────┐
│  139  J. Compensation Summary│   │     DATE           TIME       │
│  137  K. Employee Record     │   │   05/20/88       11:00:42     │
│  166  L. Inventory           │   │                               │
│  165  M. Order Log           │   │   N. Change Date              │
└──────────────────────────────┘   └──────────────────────────────┘
        ═══════[Enter Selection (A - N, or X to quit) : :]═══════
```